50 THINGS TO KNOW

ABOUT BIRDS IN THE USA

If you know someone who loves birds, I cannot imagine them not learning or enjoying this book. This book is perfect for both experienced birders and beginners alike. It is written in readable prose and studded with personal stories from the author's many years of observing birds.

50 Things to Know About Birds in Pennsylvania: Birding in the Keystone State
Author Darryl & Jackie Speicher

I really enjoyed this book. I live in the Badger state and I learned a lot of things I didn't know before. The author got me excited about taking up bird watching. Definitely going to plan a day trip to Horicon Marsh.

50 Things to Know About Birds in Wisconsin : Birding in the Badger State
Author Carly Lincoln

Smart little book for my birding friend! Includes a clever guide for regional experiences!

50 Things to Know About Birds in Florida: Birding in the Sunshine State
Author Krystal Hickey

50 THINGS TO KNOW ABOUT BIRDS IN TENNESSEE

Birding in the Volunteer State

Sarah Flanagan

Cover designed by: Ivana Stamenkovic
Cover Image: 1. By Self. - Own work, CC BY-SA 4.0,
https://commons.wikimedia.org/w/index.php?curid=27966257 2. By TonyCastro - Own work, CC BY-
SA 4.0, https://commons.wikimedia.org/w/index.php?curid=107379590 3. By Chuck Homler d/b/a
FocusOnwWildlife - Own work, CC BY-SA 4.0,
https://commons.wikimedia.org/w/index.php?curid=150305400 4. By Ryanx7 - Own work, CC BY-SA
4.0, https://commons.wikimedia.org/w/index.php?curid=72020641 5. By Greg Hume - Own work, CC
BY-SA 3.0, https://commons.wikimedia.org/w/index.php?curid=17748634 6. By Jarkko Järvinen -
Flickr, CC BY-SA 2.0, https://commons.wikimedia.org/w/index.php?curid=44848627 7. By
Rhododendrites - Own work, CC BY-SA 4.0,
https://commons.wikimedia.org/w/index.php?curid=104543328 8. By DallasPenner - Own work, CC
BY-SA 4.0, https://commons.wikimedia.org/w/index.php?curid=148141231 9. By Larry Lamsa -
Rufous Humming Bird, CC BY 2.0, https://commons.wikimedia.org/w/index.php?curid=121323201

CZYK Publishing Since 2011.
CZYKPublishing.com
50 Things to Know
Lock Haven, PA
All rights reserved.
ISBN: 9798305670660

50 THINGS TO KNOW ABOUT BIRDS IN TENNESSEE

BOOK DESCRIPTION

Why is Tennessee one of the best places to see the fall migration of hawks and eagles? Where can I see Sandhill cranes in Tennessee? What is the state bird of Tennessee? If you find yourself asking any of these questions then this book is for you...

50 Things to Know about the Birds in Tennessee by Author Sarah Flanagan offers an elegant approach to finding the most beautiful and varied species of birds on the continent. Most books on birding tell you to travel to specific locations and hotspots for one or two prize species on your life list. Although there's nothing wrong with that, this book takes another approach. Here we present you with the regional view of the state, and help you to locate the habitats and special locations near your travel destination. From this view, we will help you find a diverse community of birds and celebrate the similarities between species. Tennessee has an extraordinary geography, and there is a great overlap in breeding and wintering ranges for many species. The state is uniquely positioned to offer a variety of habitats with irruptive specialties throughout the year. Based on knowledge from the world's leading experts, understanding the role birds play in their habitat brings a greater appreciation to the art of bird watching.

This book will help you learn which habitats you should visit to find the species you are most interested in, such as warblers, thrushes, sparrows, and raptors. There are also helpful hints for making some of the more challenging bird identifications. By the time you finish this book, you will know .... So grab YOUR copy today. You'll be glad you did.

TABLE OF CONTENTS

27. American Kestrel

28. Eastern Kingbird

29. Barn Swallow

30. Yellow Warbler

31. Indigo Bunting

32. Painted Bunting

33. Western Meadowlark

34. Red-Winged Blackbird

35. Black Bellied Whistling Duck

36. Mute Swan

37. Muscovy Duck

38. American Wigeon

39. Northern Shoveler

40. Bufflehead

41. Common Loon

42. Common Merganser

43. Pied Billed Grebe

44. American White Pelican

45. Double Crested Cormorant

46. Great Blue Heron

47. Cattle Egret

48. Glossy Ibis

49. Wood Stork

50. American Coot

Other Resources:

50 Things to Know About Birds in the United States Books

ABOUT THE AUTHOR

Sarah Flanagan lives on a small homestead in the North Georgia Mountains. When she isn't homeschooling her daughter, she is probably playing with her menagerie of animals or writing children's books under the name Katherine Bartlett. Under her own name, Sarah has written 2 cookbooks, a travel book and a variety of magazine articles. Some of her work can be seen in Willow and Sage & Backwoods Home Magazine. Sarah also currently studies Ornithology with Cornell University. You can follow her author site at katherinebartlettbooks.weebly.com and on Instagram @kbwhiskey

DEDICATION

This book is dedicated to my daughter, Mary. We both have a love of nature and animals that compliment each other.

INTRODUCTION

*"There is but one kind of love; God is love,
and all his creatures derive theirs from his; only it
is modified by the different degrees of intelligence
in different beings and creatures."*

- John James Audubon

For years I have always had a fascination with birds. I'll never forget when I was pregnant with my daughter, Mary, I was standing outside on my back porch one day. All of a sudden I heard the flapping of wings that was so loud that it actually scared me. At first I had no idea what had happened but it was when I looked over at my husband and saw a tame parakeet sitting on his shoulder did I realize it was just a little bird. The tame parakeet was lost and saw us as a refuge and a place of safety. We never did find its owners so we ended up adopting it ourselves. And because of that little parakeet I found a love for birds I never knew I had.

Birds are such fascinating creatures and are so intelligent. Over the years we ended up having a house full of birds that amounted to over 15. We spent so much time with them and started to notice all their personalities were different, just like people. They each had likes, dislikes and even quirks about them. Most people wouldn't think that of birds but if you just spend enough time with them, you can see that they aren't so different from us after all.

I truly hope you enjoy this book and find the tips helpful on your own journey to learning about birds in Tennessee.

WOODLAND BIRDS OF TENNESSEE

1. EASTERN SCREECH OWL

Eastern screech owls are small but charismatic birds. One of the most iconic of the owls, with its signature tufted ears, this nocturnal creature generally stands between 6 to 10 inches tall and has a wingspan of around 18 to 24 inches. The color of its plumage ranges from gray to reddish-brown, and this helps it to conceal itself against tree bark very effectively, since it's a superb cryptic color.

Eastern screech owls are some of the most adaptable creatures you'll find living in all sorts of habitats, from hardwood forests to city parks and suburban neighborhoods. In the south, this is an owl you will most likely hear in the middle of the night! They like places with a combination of open ground and wooded habitat, where they can hunt for their primary food: small mammals, birds, and insects. They will be heard at night, both in the trill and screech ranges of sound for a communication medium that is very similar to what we would think of as territory marking.

Owls are mostly solitary and extremely territorial, roosting during the day in tree holes or thick brush. Their active time however, is at night as hunters and therefore have excellent hearing and are able to see in the dark enabling them to find prey. Their trademark hunting strategy involves perching and waiting for an unsuspecting animal to pass by.

The Eastern screech owl, for example, can be heard virtually anywhere you go in Tennessee — from rural woodlands to city parks. Our family personally hears them a lot in the woods across from us. They are often found in a wide range of environments due to their adaptability to human-impacted surroundings. These owls, drab and sometimes very well camouflaged against tree bark, provide a challenge for birdwatchers (although many get pleasure just from spotting the birds).

Specific Places to Find Eastern Screech Owls in Tennessee

Look for Eastern Screech Owls in places with second growth forests like:

Great Smoky Mountains National Park: This area's extensive tree cover creates a variety of habitats.

Shelby Farms Park in Memphis: Features partly wooded areas and many open spaces.

Radnor Lake State Park in Nashville: Has a mix of forests and bodies of water that attract owls.

2. COOPER'S HAWK

Are you ready to meet an incredible bird of prey? This broad-chest middle-sized hawk is named in honor of the naturalist William Cooper and with its long-tail and sharp-talons it needs little effort to chase down all types of prey. Cooper's hawks are medium-sized raptors that range from small to plump as adults. It takes a little practice to be able to identify them from the air but it's worth it when you do see one. The plumage is blue-gray on the back, with reddish barring on the chest and a white belly. This means they camouflage perfectly into their forest habitats and helps with one of the most critical aspects when hunting.

Cooper's hawks may inhabit a variety of settings from undisturbed deciduous and mixed forests, to urban and suburban settings. They do best in regions with sufficient tree cover, giving them nesting locations and places to hunt. While their diet is almost exclusively birds, they are also known to prey on small mammals as well, making these adaptable hunters. These incredible creatures have marked agility and speed, enabling them to navigate thick foliage, where they can pounce as a surprise on unsuspecting prey!

Across Tennessee, we see Cooper's hawks in a range of places — from city parks to state wildlife refuges. They are beautiful to watch as they fly through the air. They are most active in spring breeding season, and often observed hunting by bird feeders in suburbs. Birdwatchers admire the Cooper's hawk for its good looks and behavior since this bird plays an essential role in our ecosystem.

Specific Places to Find the Cooper's Hawk in Tennessee
Urban and Suburban Areas

Nashville: Parks like Centennial Park and Shelby Bottoms Greenway often have Cooper's hawks hunting near bird feeders.

Memphis: Overton Park and Shelby Farms Park are great locations for birdwatching.

State Parks and Natural Areas

Radnor Lake State Park (Nashville): This park has dense woodlands and is a good spot for observing various bird species, including Cooper's hawks.

Harrison Bay State Park (near Chattanooga): This park features forests and open areas, making it suitable for spotting raptors.

Pickwick Landing State Park (near Counce): A mix of woodlands and lakeside habitats can attract Cooper's hawks.

Wildlife Refuges

Tennessee National Wildlife Refuge (near Paris): This refuge provides diverse habitats, ideal for raptors.

Chickasaw National Wildlife Refuge (near Ripley): The varied landscapes here support a range of wildlife, including Cooper's hawks.

3. RUFFED GROUSE

The ruffed grouse is among the unique birds that inhabit North America in terms of adaptability and certain behaviors. In general, they are found in areas with a lot of mixed-species woodlands. This medium game bird can be roughly 16 to 20 inches in length. Gray shades compose the plumage; this serves as camouflage with the leaf-littered bottom of the forest for predator evasion.

The ruffed grouse are very fascinating to observe with regard to their courtship behavior during the mating season. The male ruffed grouses have a "drumming" display of sound, which is one of the methods produced by wing beats while perched atop a log or rock. This rhythmic beat can echo through the forest, signaling to partners their location. It is not an exclusive ritual for mating but also serves as a declaration of territory because males lay claim and protect their breeding grounds from challengers.

The plant composition of leaves, buds, and seeds is the preferred diet of ruffed grouses during spring and summer. During winter, they shift to buds and twigs of trees and shrubs. It further manifests their adaptability that they are able to alter their diets inter-seasonally. They also have another behavior called "snow roostin"; they burrow into the snow for warmth and safety during nights in winter.

This isn't a typical bird to find our roaming so spotting one in the wild is very special.

Specific Places to Find the Ruffed Grouse in Tennessee

Great Smoky Mountains National Park

This vast park features diverse habitats, including mixed deciduous and coniferous forests, which are ideal for ruffed grouse. Look in areas with dense underbrush and young forests.

Cherokee National Forest

The Cherokee National Forest, located in southeastern Tennessee, offers a mix of habitats that support ruffed grouse. Check areas around the Ocoee River and in the higher elevations.

Roan Mountain State Park

Known for its beautiful landscapes and hiking trails, Roan Mountain State Park has suitable forested areas where ruffed grouse can be found.

Prentice Cooper State Forest

Located near Chattanooga, this state forest has a mix of mature woodlands and younger growth, providing a habitat for ruffed grouse.

Catoosa Wildlife Management Area

This area offers a variety of habitats, including forests and open lands. It's a good spot for hunting and observing ruffed grouse.

Bledsoe State Forest

This state forest features diverse woodlands and is known to support ruffed grouse populations. It's located in East Tennessee, making it accessible for birdwatchers and hunters.

Land Between the Lakes National Recreation Area

While primarily in Kentucky and a small portion in Tennessee, this area provides suitable habitats for ruffed grouse, particularly in forested sections.

4. YELLOW-BILLED CUCKOO

The yellow-billed cuckoo is one of those interesting birds that, besides having a generally interesting look, is also famous for its curiosities. This medium-sized bird, about 11 to 12 inches in length, can be easily recognized due to its long, slender body, bright yellow bill, and striking plumage: the back is olive brown, and the underparts are white with dark spots. With this in mind it will fit right into its woodland surroundings. The yellow-billed cuckoo is more often heard than seen; its call—a series of rhythmic "cu-coo" sounds—echoes through the trees, especially during the breeding season. Their beautiful call is lovely to hear while you're out searching for birds.

Preferred habitats for yellow-billed cuckoos range from open woodlands to riparian areas, including dense shrubs, where there is abundant food and nesting sites. They are associated with water because they feed mostly on caterpillars, insects, and fruits. They especially favor tent caterpillars, avoided by many birds because of the toxins that they carry. Such a diet allows yellow-billed cuckoos to exploit an environment which may be hostile to other species.

During the breeding season, which generally occurs late in the spring and into early summer, males execute extravagant courtship displays, using calls and brilliant bills to attract females. Nesting is in dense foliage and females lay three to five eggs. The chicks are altricial, surviving on their parents for food and protection until they fledge.

The Yellow-billed Cuckoo is a common, and generally more abundant in eastern Tennessee, migrant through the state. Most birds migrate to Central America and South America for the nonbreeding season.

Specific Places to Find the Yellow-Billed Cuckoo in Tennessee

Great Smoky Mountains National Park

This expansive park features diverse ecosystems, including dense forests and riparian areas where yellow-billed cuckoos can be found. Look for them along streams and in areas with abundant foliage.

Reelfoot Lake State Park

Known for its wetlands and wooded areas, Reelfoot Lake provides an ideal habitat for yellow-billed cuckoos, especially during migration and the breeding season.

Land Between the Lakes National Recreation Area

This area has a mix of forested habitats and open spaces, offering suitable environments for cuckoos. Explore the wooded areas along the lakes and riverbanks.

Radnor Lake State Park

Located near Nashville, this park has rich woodlands and a lake, making it a good spot for birdwatching. The lush vegetation provides excellent cover for yellow-billed cuckoos.

Cherokee National Forest

This national forest features a variety of habitats, including mixed deciduous forests where yellow-billed cuckoos can thrive. Focus on areas near water sources for the best chances of spotting them.

Shelby Farms Park

In Memphis, this large urban park has a mix of natural areas and open fields. Cuckoos can be found in the wooded regions and along the park's water features.

Cumberland River Greenway

This greenway in Nashville has riparian habitats that attract yellow-billed cuckoos, especially during migration and breeding seasons.

5. RUFOUS HUMMINGBIRD

The rufous hummingbird is one of the spectacular species of hummingbirds, and most people identify with the spectacular view of the species' bright coloration and energetic behavior. Measuring around 3 to 4 inches, they possess brilliant orange and green plumage, especially the unmistakable colors on the male, which have a gorgeous iridescent throat known as a gorget. This makes the rufous hummingbird one of North America's most visually appealing birds.

Rufous hummingbirds are endemic to the western United States and parts of Canada. They are also celebrated for their extraordinary migrations from their breeding grounds in the Pacific Northwest to wintering areas in Mexico as it's considered to have completed an extraordinary journey. In fact, Rufous hummingbirds travel over 3,000 miles while migrating-this is the longest migration of all hummingbird species. While migrating, rufous hummingbirds were found to be aggressive in defending territories around feeding sites from other birds, as they vigorously fought over them.

Rufous hummingbirds feed on nectar from several flowering plants, including trumpet vine and columbine. This allows them to probe deeply into flowers using their specialized long bills that have arrows that extend along the sides to collect nectar drops deep within flowers, along with an extendible tongue to lap up nectar drops. To hover and maneuver in such precision, they beat their wings rapidly. They also eat small insects and spiders as a source of protein besides nectar.

Rufous hummingbirds are occasionally seen in Tennessee during migration, most often when passing through during the spring and fall. Apparently, it's rich nectar flowers or feeders with sugar-water solution that may attract them to the garden. Watching these brilliant birds is many people's delight simply for the speed of their flight and the attractive colors they display that give life to any garden. It appears that Rufous hummingbirds can only be seen during migration, chiefly in the spring and fall.

To add to your chances of seeing a Rufous hummingbird, make sure to hang hummingbird feeders and keep them filled with hummingbird food in spring.

Specific Places to Find the Rufous Hummingbird in Tennessee

Great Smoky Mountains National Park

The park's diverse flora attracts a variety of hummingbirds, including rufous hummingbirds during migration. Look for them in flowering areas, especially near streams and meadows.

Radnor Lake State Park

Located near Nashville, this park offers suitable habitats with abundant flowering plants. Hummingbird feeders can attract rufous hummingbirds in migration seasons.

Shelby Farms Park

This large urban park in Memphis has a mix of woodlands and meadows. Setting up feeders here can draw rufous hummingbirds, especially in spring and fall.

Cumberland River Greenway

This greenway in Nashville features riparian habitats with plenty of flowers, making it a good spot for observing migrating hummingbirds.

Reelfoot Lake State Park

Known for its wetlands and diverse plant life, Reelfoot Lake can be a great location to spot rufous hummingbirds during migration periods.

Hatchie National Wildlife Refuge

Located near Brownsville, this refuge has various habitats that can attract migrating hummingbirds, especially around flowering plants.

Local Gardens and Backyards

Many bird enthusiasts successfully attract rufous hummingbirds by setting up nectar feeders filled with a sugar-water solution. Planting native, nectar-rich flowers in gardens can also draw them in during migration.

6. YELLOW-BELLIED SAPSUCKER

Interesting among woodpeckers, due to their feeding habits and striking appearance, the yellow-bellied sapsucker is a sight to see. This medium-sized bird, about 7 to 9 inches long, sports bold black and white markings, including a distinctive yellow-colored belly from which it takes its name. Males are especially identifiable with their bright red throats, in which females are more subdued in coloration, evidencing sexual dimorphism in most birds.

The yellow-bellied sapsuckers breed over much of North America, ranging from the eastern part northwards. They make use of varied woodland habitats, which range from deciduous forests to mixed woodlands and even suburban areas. The most distinctive feature of their behavior is the unique foraging strategy that involves pecking small holes into tree bark to allow them to feed on the sap, together with insects attracted to the resource. This behavior provides them not only with food, but it is also a valuable resource for other birds and wildlife that benefit from the sap flow.

During the breeding season-roughly late March to July, yellow-bellied sapsuckers establish territories and attract mates with their distinct drumming and vocalizations. Nesting is done in tree cavities; a clutch of eggs will be laid which the parents will incubate and take care of after it hatches.

In Tennessee, yellow-bellied sapsuckers are generally only seen during spring and fall migration as they move between their Canadian breeding grounds and wintering grounds in the southern United States. Birdwatchers can maximize their chances to see these charismatic woodpeckers by searching woodlands with plenty of trees, especially near sap-producing species such as maples and birches. Our family has been able to spot many of them in the woods behind our home.

Specific Locations to Find the Yellow-Bellied Sapsucker in Tennessee

Great Smoky Mountains National Park

This national park offers diverse habitats with abundant deciduous trees, making it a prime spot for yellow-bellied sapsuckers, especially during migration.

Cherokee National Forest

This forest features a variety of tree species, including maples and birches, which attract sapsuckers. Look for them in mixed woodlands and along trails.

Radnor Lake State Park

Located near Nashville, this park has rich wooded areas and water sources, creating an inviting habitat for migrating yellow-bellied sapsuckers.

Reelfoot Lake State Park

The wetland and forested areas around Reelfoot Lake provide a suitable environment for yellow-bellied sapsuckers during their migratory stopovers.

Land Between the Lakes National Recreation Area

This area has a mix of forest types and is known for its birdwatching opportunities. Sapsuckers can often be found in the wooded sections during migration.

Cumberland River Greenway

This greenway in Nashville features riparian habitats that can attract yellow-bellied sapsuckers, especially in spring and fall.

Local Parks and Urban Woodlands

Many city parks and urban areas with mature trees, such as Shelby Farms Park in Memphis, can provide good opportunities to spot these birds during migration.

7. EASTERN WOOD-PEWEE

The eastern wood-pewee is a small, inconspicuous flycatcher identified by its distinct call and range of wooded habitats. The bird is about 6 to 7 inches in length, gray-brown in color, and can easily blend into its surroundings. Its subtle beauty is accentuated with a relatively long tail and pale yellowish belly, hence a beautiful sight to behold for a keen observer.

Eastern wood-pewees range mainly throughout eastern North America; preferred habitats include deciduous and mixed forests, mostly around open woodlands or edges. If you live in the woods like we do, you might see some in your own backyard! Through its breeding season, in late spring to early summer, the birds establish territories and go through dramatic displays to lure a mate. They are characterized by their call, an eerie "pee-wee" among the forest, hence the name for this bird. This is not only a call, but it also serves as territorial marking against other intruders.

Eastern wood-pewees mostly feed on insects, which they catch in mid-air with fantastic agility. They may be seen perched on low branches or wires, where they patiently wait until darting out to catch their prey. Thus, their foraging strategy is quite patient and precisely accurate to ensure success in the forested environments.

In Tennessee, eastern wood-pewees are most commonly observed in the state throughout the breeding season when birds can be found in areas with woods such as state parks and national forests.

Specific Locations to Find the Eastern Wood-Pewee in Tennessee
Great Smoky Mountains National Park

This vast park offers a range of habitats, including deciduous forests and open woodlands. Look for eastern wood-pewees along hiking trails and near streams.

Cherokee National Forest

The diverse ecosystems in this national forest provide ideal habitats for eastern wood-pewees. Focus on areas with mixed hardwoods and open canopies.

Radnor Lake State Park

Located near Nashville, this park features wooded areas and water sources. Eastern wood-pewees can often be heard calling from the trees.

Shelby Farms Park

In Memphis, this large park includes a mix of natural areas and woodlands, making it a good spot for observing eastern wood-pewees during migration and the breeding season.

Cumberland River Greenway

This greenway in Nashville offers riparian habitats and wooded edges, which can attract eastern wood-pewees. Keep an ear out for their distinctive calls.

Reelfoot Lake State Park

The park's wetland and forested areas provide suitable habitats for many bird species, including the eastern wood-pewee, especially during the breeding season.

Local Nature Reserves and Parks

Many local parks with mature trees, such as Percy Warner Park in Nashville, can also be good locations to spot eastern wood-pewees.

8. EASTERN PHEBE

The eastern phebe is a charming, adaptable flycatcher with a native range to North America. About 6-8 inches long, it is basically a grayish-brown bird above and pale below, with a tail that is very distinctive since it is somewhat forked. Its subdued plumage makes it somewhat unobtrusive; its presence, though, is often betrayed by a very distinctive call—a sharp, two-note "phebe," which names the bird but also advertises its territory.

Eastern phebes are typically found in open woodlands, fields, and urban areas. These birds enjoy these areas since they present them with ample opportunity for hunting insects near water. They have a peculiar way of hunting for food by perching onto low branches or fences after which they dart out to catch flying insects right in mid-air. They typically feed on flies, moths, and beetles, showing just how agile and quick these birds are.

The nesting, which usually happens from late March to August, is done so in a protected area most of the time from man-made objects:

on or under bridges, barns, and around porches. The adaptation to the urban environment is one of the reasons why these phoebes are thriving and increasing their numbers in many areas. The female then lays four to five eggs that she alone incubates for two weeks until they hatch.

In Tennessee, eastern phebes are common, and their range encompasses every part of the state during the warmer months. They are very fascinating to watch but keep your eyes peeled: they fly fast!

Specific Locations to Find the Eastern Phebe in Tennessee

- **Great Smoky Mountains National Park**: Look along streams and rivers, especially in areas like Cades Cove and the Oconaluftee Visitor Center.

- **Radnor Lake State Park (Nashville)**: This park has wooded areas and water, making it a good spot for spotting Eastern Phebes.

- **Reelfoot Lake State Park**: This area is great for birdwatching, particularly near the water.

- **Shelby Farms Park (Memphis)**: With its varied habitats, this large park often has Eastern Phebes in the spring and fall.

- **Tennessee River Gorge**: Explore the trails and edges of this area for opportunities to see these birds.

- **Cheatham Wildlife Management Area**: This WMA offers diverse habitats where Eastern Phebes can be found.

- **Nashville's Urban Parks**: Parks like Centennial Park and Fort Negley can attract Eastern Phebes, especially in migration seasons.

9. RED-EYED VIREO

One of the identifying characteristics of the restless little bird known as the Red-eyed Vireo, resident over most of North America and an abundant breeder in the eastern United States and parts of Canada, is its olive-green back, pale underparts, and conspicuous red eyes. Subtly beautiful, this captures the imagination of a serious bird watcher just as much as it can for the casual bird observer.

The Red-eyed Vireo is approximately 5.5 to 6.5 inches long, with a stout body and its thick, hooked bill, typical of insectivorous birds. During the breeding season, this species favors deciduous and mixed forests to nest in, mostly in understory. Their intricately woven nests of plant fibers are firmly attached to the branches, showing their remarkable skills in building. Finding their nests is fun because you can see just how amazing they are!

But perhaps the most distinctive feature of the Red-eyed Vireo, though, is its intricate song-a series of melodious phrases that often seems a question: "Here I am, where are you? " Almost synonymous with its presence in the forest, especially during spring and summer, is the song sung by males to claim territory and lure mates.

The Red-eyed Vireo also has an incredible singing talent, with estimates for some individuals to sing up to over twenty song types. The Red-eyed Vireo migrates to Central America, returning to North America in the spring.

Specific Locations to Find the Red-Eyed Vireo in Tennessee

- **Great Smoky Mountains National Park:** Explore the park's diverse habitats, especially along trails like the Alum Cave Trail and the Roaring Fork Motor Nature Trail, where they are often found in understory vegetation.

- **Radnor Lake State Park (Nashville)**: This park features woodlands and trails that are great for spotting Red-eyed Vireos during the spring and summer.

- **Shelby Farms Park (Memphis)**: With its mix of woodlands and wetlands, this large urban park can be a good place to hear and see these birds.

- **Cherokee Park (Knoxville)**: This park has a variety of habitats, including forests and edges, where Red-eyed Vireos can be found singing.

- **Cumberland Gap National Historical Park**: The park's diverse plant life provides excellent nesting and feeding opportunities for Red-eyed Vireos.

- **Tennessee River Gorge**: The wooded areas along the gorge are excellent for birdwatching, particularly during migration.

- **Land Between the Lakes National Recreation Area**: This area offers a mix of forests and open spaces, making it a good spot for various bird species, including the Red-eyed Vireo.

10. BLUE JAY

The Blue Jay is a strikingly beautiful bird native to North America, instantly recognizable by its bright blue plumage, white underparts, and characteristic black necklace-like collar. With a wingspan of about 13 to 17 inches, the Blue Jay is an intelligent and highly social bird; hence, this makes it a very interesting subject among all bird enthusiasts.

Blue Jays appear in forests and parks, and they might easily inhabit suburban areas, as they are relatively adaptable to a number of disparate habitats. Our family often seeing Blue Jays in our yard. Their diet is omnivorous, with the main components being acorns, seeds, fruits, insects, and sometimes small vertebrates. They also serve an important purpose in their ecosystem as seed dispersers, especially oak trees, because they continually hoard acorns for future use. This behavior not only serves to support their survival but at the same time aids in forest regeneration.

One of the most remarkable features of the Blue Jay is their vocal capability. They utter all kinds of calls, from sharp whistles to loud screeches, even down to the imitation of other birds, such as that of hawks. Their call mimicking is a way of communication and a warning system used to alert other birds of potential dangers.

No less fabled are the social dynamics of the Blue Jays: They often travel in little family groups and can be quite aggressive when defending their territory. Their intelligence shows in the ways they solve problems and adapt to, even urban environments, where they frequently scrounge for food.

Specific Locations to Find the Blue Jay in Tennessee

- **Great Smoky Mountains National Park:** Look for Blue Jays in the park's diverse habitats, particularly near picnic areas and along trails like the Alum Cave Trail.

- **Radnor Lake State Park (Nashville)**: This park features wooded areas where Blue Jays are frequently spotted, especially near feeding stations.

- **Shelby Farms Park (Memphis)**: With its mix of woodlands and open areas, this large park provides excellent opportunities for observing Blue Jays.

- **Cheatham Wildlife Management Area**: This area has a variety of habitats, making it a good spot for birdwatching, including Blue Jays.

- **Percy Warner Park (Nashville)**: The wooded trails and open fields here are ideal for spotting these vibrant birds.

39

- **Long Hunter State Park**: Explore the trails along the shores of J. Percy Priest Lake, where Blue Jays can often be seen foraging.

- **Cumberland Gap National Historical Park**: The park's forests and meadows provide excellent habitats for Blue Jays, especially during the warmer months.

- **Local Gardens and Parks**: Many suburban areas with mature trees, such as local parks and gardens, often attract Blue Jays.

11. FISH CROW

The Fish Crow is a medium-sized bird native to the southeastern United States in particular, along the coast and river systems. It is identified by its all-black plumage, stout body, and slightly smaller size compared to the more common American Crow. The Fish Crow is an interesting member of the corvid family due to its intelligence and adaptability.

Generally 15 to 20 inches in length, the Fish Crow is commonly found near any form of water, from estuaries and marshes to rivers. They feed on aquatic life: fish, crustaceans, and mollusks, which their name would suggest. Fish Crows are opportunistic foragers and can often be seen scavenging along shorelines or thieving from other birds. The ability to exploit various sources of food involves an ecological function as predator and scavenger alike.

The most distinctive feature of the Fish Crow relates to its vocalization, including a series of cawing sounds, which are often described as a more nasal and much softer "caw" than those made by the American Crow. This would enable birdwatchers to differentiate between the birds in the wild easily if heard. But it might take practice to identify them by sight alone. Socially, Fish Crows are seen in small groups, sometimes out of the breeding season, playing with others and partaking in complicated social interactions.

As for their habitat, Fish Crows tend to like an open area with abundant water and sufficient supplies of food. They are commonly seen within littoral areas, wetlands, and even in towns where humans increase access to food.

Specific Locations to Find the Fish Crow in Tennessee

- **Shelby Farms Park (Memphis):** This large park includes wetlands and lakes, making it a great spot for observing Fish Crows.

- **Meeman-Shelby Forest State Park**: Located near the Mississippi River, this park's diverse habitats are suitable for Fish Crows.

- **Reelfoot Lake State Park**: This area is known for its wetlands and abundant wildlife, including Fish Crows, especially around the lake's edges.

- **Tennessee River**: Areas along the Tennessee River, particularly near towns like Chattanooga and Knoxville, can attract Fish Crows, especially in the summer.

- **Nashville's Riverfront Park**: The urban waterfront environment provides good feeding opportunities for Fish Crows, often seen foraging near the water.

- **Land Between the Lakes National Recreation Area**: This area features a mix of habitats near water, ideal for spotting Fish Crows.

- **Harrison Bay State Park**: Located near Chattanooga, this park has lakes and rivers where Fish Crows can be seen foraging.

- **Wetlands and Marshes**: Look for Fish Crows in other local wetlands and marsh areas, especially during migration seasons.

12. BLACK-CAPPED CHICKADEE

The Black-capped Chickadee is a small, non-migratory songbird instantly recognized by its distinctive black cap and bib with white cheeks on a soft gray body. I always love seeing when they visit my yard. In my opinion, they are some of the cutest backyard birds because of their tiny stature and bold temperment. About 4.5 to 5.5 inches long, this charismatic bird is very common over North America, especially in the eastern and northern parts, inhabiting forests, parks, and backyards alike.

The most characteristic feature of the Black-capped Chickadee is its call-a clear, cheerily whistled "chick-a-dee-dee-dee", which escalates in rate and intensity when a predator is sensed. In such cases, this call serves as a warning call to the other birds regarding an imminent danger. The number of "dee" notes tacked onto the end of the call is directly proportional to the amount of threat; this shows their quite advanced capabilities for communication.

These birds are very social; during the non-breeding season, they are usually seen in a mixed-species flock and feed together. Feeding mostly consists of seeds, insects, and berries. The Black-capped Chickadees are remarkable for their foraging behavior-they can hang upside down in search of food and are great in caching seeds for later use.

Regarding nesting, the Black-capped Chickadee takes a tree cavity or artificial nest box and lays 5 to 13 eggs in a clutch. It is a very stable, firm family unit, as far as raising the young is concerned as both parents are engaged.

Specific Locations to Find the Black-Capped Chickadee in Tennessee

Great Smoky Mountains National Park: Explore areas like Cades Cove and the park's numerous trails, where chickadees are commonly seen in mixed forests.

- **Radnor Lake State Park (Nashville):** This park features wooded trails that provide excellent habitat for Black-capped Chickadees, especially near feeding stations.

- **Shelby Farms Park (Memphis):** The diverse habitats in this large urban park attract various bird species, including chickadees.

- **Chattanooga Arboretum and Nature Center:** This area offers a mix of gardens and natural habitats, making it a good spot for observing Black-capped Chickadees.

- **Long Hunter State Park:** The park's forests along J. Percy Priest Lake provide great opportunities to spot these charming birds.

- **Cumberland Gap National Historical Park:** The park's varied habitats, including forests and fields, are conducive to sightings of Black-capped Chickadees.

- **Local Parks and Backyards:** Many suburban areas with trees and feeders, such as neighborhood parks and gardens, often attract Black-capped Chickadees.

13. TUFTED TITMOUSE

The Tufted Titmouse is a tiny, non-migratory songbird native to eastern and central North America. It is unmistakably distinguished by its tufted crown, gray plumage, and warm orange flanks. This was one of the first birds I learned about when I started birdwatching. In the south, not many grey birds have a little tufted head! This cute bird measures about 5.5 to 6.5 inches in length. The tuft on its head endows this bird with a curious and vivacious personality that charms both birders and nature lovers alike.

It inhabits different types of habitats, from deciduous and mixed forests to suburban gardens and parks. Often in company with other bird species, the Tufted Titmouse forms flocks in mixed species during the non-breeding season. It feeds on seeds, insects, and berries, which are obtained by foraging among the branches and foliage. This species is an acrobatic forager since it can hang upside down when obtaining food-a manifestation of its agility and adaptability.

One of the striking features of the Tufted Titmouse is its vocalization. The bird gives a distinctive whistled call, often expressed as "peter-peter-peter." Such a call not only serves as a method of communication between individuals but also aids in establishing territory and attracting mates during the breeding season. Nesting often occurs in tree cavities; raising their offspring is a shared responsibility for both parents, which shows a very strong familial bond.

The Tufted Titmouse are year-round residents throughout their range, and are a favorite renter for many bird fanciers, as they can be very docile and feeder-friendly. They can often and easily become a commonplace visitor to one's yard if sunflower seeds or peanuts are put out and consumed.

Specific Locations to Find the Tufted Titmouse in Tennessee

- **Great Smoky Mountains National Park:** Look for them in wooded areas and along trails like the Roaring Fork Motor Nature Trail and Cades Cove.

- **Radnor Lake State Park (Nashville)**: This park has mixed forests and is a great spot for observing Tufted Titmice, especially near feeders.

- **Shelby Farms Park (Memphis)**: The diverse habitats of this large park provide good opportunities to see Tufted Titmice among other songbirds.

- **Long Hunter State Park**: Explore the trails near J. Percy Priest Lake, where Tufted Titmice are commonly seen.

- **Chattanooga Arboretum and Nature Center**: This area has a mix of gardens and natural habitats, making it a good spot for spotting these birds.

- **Cumberland Gap National Historical Park**: The park's varied ecosystems, including forests and open spaces, are conducive to sightings of Tufted Titmice.

14. RED-BREASTED NUTHATCH

The Red-breasted Nuthatch is a tiny, energetic bird with an astonishing streak of color and an effervescent personality. Distinctive features of this nuthatch are a slate-blue back, rusty orange underparts, and a black cap. It resides primarily in coniferous forests across North America and has been quite common in the western regions of the country and at higher elevations throughout the eastern United States in winter.

The Red-breasted Nuthatches are quite adapted birds and can often be seen foraging on tree trunks and branches, showing their classic behavior of climbing headfirst down trees. They are super cute to watch for all ages too! Their diet consists mainly of seeds, especially from conifers, but also includes insects and berries. They are well noted for their habit of caching food, storing seeds in crevices of bark or under scales of pine cones, to be eaten later. These actions not only enable them to live through severe winters but also contribute to the regeneration process in forests since part of the cached seeds may grow into new trees.

Most characteristic, however, and the most distinctive call of the Red-breasted Nuthatch is its nasal "yank-yank", which is very commonly heard in coniferous forests. These birds have a lot of reasons for this call; it may be an alarm call or a territorial one. During the breeding season, it builds nests in tree cavities, often sealing the entrance with sap to protect its young from predators.

Specific Locations to Find the Red-Breasted Nuthatch in Tennessee

- **Great Smoky Mountains National Park:** This park's higher elevations, especially around the Cataloochee Valley and Clingmans Dome, are ideal habitats for Red-breasted Nuthatches, particularly in coniferous forests.

- **Roan Mountain State Park**: The spruce-fir forests on Roan Mountain provide suitable habitat for these nuthatches, especially during migration.

- **Cherokee National Forest**: Explore the areas with mixed forests and conifer stands, particularly along the trails where Red-breasted Nuthatches are often found foraging.

- **Cumberland Gap National Historical Park**: The park's diverse forest habitats, including coniferous areas, make it a good spot for spotting these birds.

- **Long Hunter State Park**: Look for Red-breasted Nuthatches in the wooded areas near J. Percy Priest Lake, especially during the winter months.

- **Local Nature Reserves**: Parks with mature trees and conifers, such as Percy Warner Park in Nashville, can also attract Red-breasted Nuthatches.

15. BROWN CREEPER

The Brown Creeper is a small, secretive bird with quite remarkable foraging behavior and cryptic plumage. About 5 to 6 inches long, the Brown Creeper has a lean body, long tail, and mottled brown-and-white plumage that offer spectacular camouflage against tree bark. It takes a keen eye to spot the Brown Creeper so keep your eyes peeled. This nuthatch-like bird is quite common in most forests of North America, especially in coniferous and mixed woodlands.

Of particular interest is the foraging behavior of the Brown Creeper, which is quite unlike that of most birds. The Brown Creeper spirals up the trunks, using its stiff, pointed tail for support. During its upward climb, it probes into crevices and beneath loose bark, searching for insects and larvae, besides tree sap. This behavior will allow the bird not only to find its food but also point out its specific adaptation to life in a forest environment.

One can often hear a soft, high-pitched trill of the Brown Creeper in its song throughout the breeding season. Although they are essentially solitary or in pairs, they may join mixed-species foraging flocks during winter, allowing them to exploit communal foraging opportunities. Nesting typically occurs in tree cavities or under loose bark, where females lay a clutch of 3 to 7 eggs.

Throughout much of its range, the Brown Creeper is a year-round resident and faces threats due to habitat loss and logging practices that remove older forests. Yet it can be found within urban parks when mature trees are present, and it can be fairly accessible to birdwatchers.

Specific Locations to Find the Brown Creeper in Tennessee

Great Smoky Mountains National Park: This park's diverse forest habitats, particularly in areas like Cades Cove and along trails such as the Alum Cave Trail, are excellent for spotting Brown Creepers.

- **Roan Mountain State Park**: The coniferous forests on Roan Mountain provide suitable habitat, especially during the cooler months when they are more active.

- **Cherokee National Forest**: Look for Brown Creepers in the mixed woodlands and along hiking trails, where they are often seen foraging on tree trunks.

- **Long Hunter State Park**: The wooded areas near J. Percy Priest Lake offer good opportunities for spotting these elusive birds.

- **Cumberland Gap National Historical Park**: The park's diverse habitats include old-growth forests that are ideal for Brown Creepers.

- **Radnor Lake State Park (Nashville)**: This park features mature trees and wooded trails that can attract Brown Creepers, especially in the winter.

- **Local Nature Reserves and Parks**: Look for Brown Creepers in any mature wooded areas or parks with large trees, such as Percy Warner Park in Nashville or Shelby Farms Park in Memphis.

16. WINTER WREN

The Winter Wren is a small, secretive songbird; its interesting appearance combined with energetic behavior is a lure for bird watchers and nature lovers alike. About 4 to 5 inches in length, this little wren has a short tail and slim body in rich brown plumage, often marked by slight streaking, with a lighter belly. Because of their little size and cryptic coloration, they easily disappear into the shadowy ambiance of their surroundings.

Winter Wrens are essentially birds of heavy underbrush, thickets, and riparian areas; they prefer locales with good cover. They may be residents in some parts year-round, but in the eastern United States, where they migrate south from northern grounds to winter, they are immensely more common in the winter months. They are very hard to see since they avoid open areas, but often a loud and cheerful song, a fast series of trilling notes, betrays their presence.

Winter Wrens principally forage on or near the ground and in low vegetation, particularly taking insects, spiders, and other small invertebrates. They make energetic movements, hopping and flitting about as they probe into crevices and leaf litter for food. This adds to their acrobatic behavior, showing agility quite out of proportion to their size.

During breeding season, Winter Wrens create an elaborate nest in a sheltered location, often using moss and grasses to make the nest insular and safe for its young, such as among the roots of trees or under a tangle of rocks. We actually had a family of Winter Wrens make a nest right on our front porch in a fake plant! Small but very territorial, this bird will take on much larger species during nesting season.

Specific Locations to Find the Winter Wren in Tennessee

- **Great Smoky Mountains National Park:** Look for Winter Wrens in dense underbrush and near streams, particularly along trails like the Roaring Fork Motor Nature Trail and the Laurel Falls Trail.

- **Cherokee National Forest**: The forest's rich habitats, including thickets and riparian areas, are excellent for spotting Winter Wrens, especially near streams.

- **Radnor Lake State Park (Nashville)**: This park features a mix of wooded areas and dense brush, providing good habitat for Winter Wrens, especially in winter.

- **Long Hunter State Park**: The park's wooded trails along J. Percy Priest Lake can attract Winter Wrens, particularly in the cooler months.

- **Cumberland Gap National Historical Park**: The diverse habitats within the park, including dense forests and streams, make it a suitable spot for these elusive birds.

- **South Cumberland State Park**: Explore areas with thick undergrowth and riparian zones, where Winter Wrens are often found foraging.

- **Local Parks with Dense Vegetation**: Look for Winter Wrens in any local parks or natural areas with dense underbrush and proximity to water, such as Percy Warner Park in Nashville.

17. RUBY-CROWNED KINGLET

The Ruby-crowned Kinglet is a small, energetic songbird that is easily recognized by its striking appearance and lively behavior. The bird measures 3.5 to 4.5 inches in length, hence one of North America's tiniest birds. It is the male, however, with its intense ruby-red crown that is often retracted unless the bird is excited or agitated. Both males and females have a similar olive-green plumage, with a pale underbelly and strongly contrasting wing bars, making them exceptionally handsome but secretive in their forested habitats.

Ruby-crowned Kinglets occur in a variety of wooded environments, including both coniferous and mixed forests, as well as shrubby areas. They are migratory, breeding in northern areas of the United States and Canada, and winters in southern areas of the

United States and into Mexico. During migration, they often appear in urban parks and gardens as migrants are attracted to fruiting shrubs and trees. So if you have some fruit trees around, you might have a good chance at spotting them.

These kinglets are acrobatic foragers as they flit about foliage in pursuit of insects, spiders, and small berries and often hang upside down. Their high-pitched, cheerful song and call note join in the spring and fall landscapes as one of the pleasures, adding to territorial and communicative signals.

Nesting typically occurs in dense vegetation; females construct a small, cup-shaped nest lined with soft material. When young hatch, the male helps to feed them, thereby adopting a cooperative breeding strategy that enhances their reproductive success.

Specific Locations to Find the Ruby-Crowned Kinglet in Tennessee

- **Great Smoky Mountains National Park:** Look for them in mixed coniferous and deciduous forests, particularly along trails like the Roaring Fork Motor Nature Trail and Cades Cove.

- **Radnor Lake State Park (Nashville)**: This park features diverse habitats, including woodlands and shrubby areas, which attract Ruby-crowned Kinglets, especially during migration.

- **Shelby Farms Park (Memphis)**: The park's variety of habitats, including wooded areas and open fields, provides good opportunities to spot these small birds.

- **Long Hunter State Park**: Explore the trails along J. Percy Priest Lake, where Ruby-crowned Kinglets can be found foraging in trees and shrubs.

- **Cumberland Gap National Historical Park**: The park's diverse forested areas and riparian zones are ideal habitats for observing these kinglets.

- **Chattanooga Arboretum and Nature Center**: This area has a mix of natural habitats and gardens that can attract Ruby-crowned Kinglets, particularly in the fall and spring.

- **Local Parks and Gardens**: Many suburban parks and gardens with mature trees, such as Percy Warner Park in Nashville, can also attract these energetic birds, especially during migration seasons.

•

18. BLUE-GRAY GNATCATCHER

The Blue-gray Gnatcatcher is a small and quick bird that is always so interesting to look at due to its lovely appearance and lively behavior. About 4.5 to 5 inches in length, the tiny songbird exhibits striking blue-gray plumage, a white belly, and long, slender tails with white outer feathers, which the species is often seen to flick and fan while foraging. The male and female are somewhat similar in appearance. During the breeding season, males may possibly show a bit brighter hue.

Such gnatchers are typical for open woodlands, shrubby areas, and along forest edges, mostly near water. Being migratory birds, they spend their whole breeding season in the eastern United States and move south for winter to places such as Mexico and Central America. During migration, it's not infrequent that Blue-gray

Gnatcatchers can be seen both in gardens and urban parks, where they feed upon insects and berries.

Perhaps one of the most charming things about the Blue-gray Gnatcatcher is its energetic foraging behavior. They are truly adorable to watch. It darts from branch to branch, searching mostly for small insects, especially flies and caterpillars. Their acrobatic movements enable them to exploit dense foliage with great ease. The soft, high-pitched calls and chirping songs ring out while it makes its way through its habitat, a melodious touch to the landscape.

Specific Locations to Find the Blue-Gray Gnatcatcher

- **Great Smoky Mountains National Park:** Look for them in open woodlands and along trails, especially in areas with dense underbrush and near streams.

- **Radnor Lake State Park (Nashville):** This park features diverse habitats, including woodlands and shrubby areas, which attract Blue-gray Gnatcatchers, especially during migration.

- **Shelby Farms Park (Memphis):** The park's mix of open fields and wooded areas provides good opportunities to spot these gnatcatchers.

- **Long Hunter State Park:** Explore the trails along J. Percy Priest Lake, where Blue-gray Gnatcatchers can often be seen flitting through the trees.

- **Cumberland Gap National Historical Park:** The park's diverse habitats, including open forests and shrubby areas, are ideal for observing these birds.

- **Chattanooga Arboretum and Nature Center:** This area has a mix of gardens and natural habitats that can attract Blue-gray Gnatcatchers, particularly during the spring migration.

- **Local Parks and Gardens**: Many suburban parks and gardens with shrubby areas, such as Percy Warner Park in Nashville, can also attract these lively birds, especially during migration.

19. SWAINSON'S THRUSH

The Swainson's Thrush is a small, seldom-seen bird, with a melodious song and plumage distinctive in markings. About 6.5 to 7 inches long, this thrush is distinguished by warm brown upperparts, a spotted cream-colored breast with an olive underlying tint. These features, along with its exquisitely shaped outline, create a preferred favorite among bird watchers and nature enthusiasts alike. The Swainson's Thrush is mainly confined to the dense understory of the forest, always to the heavily vegetated parts of the riparian zones, where it forages.

This is a migratory species, breeding in the boreal forests of Canada and Alaska and wintering in Central America and parts of Mexico. On migration, the Swainson's Thrush can often be found within a variety of different habitats including parks and gardens and even urban areas, resting and feeding on its way. They also feed on insects and berries with foraging taking place on the ground and in the foliage of trees and shrubs.

But one of the most interesting things about the Swainson's Thrush might be its song: a full, melodic series of notes resounding through the forest. This beautiful vocalization also serves to establish territory during the breeding season and attracts mates. Calls are often described as soft with an ethereal quality; at times, at dawn and dusk, it adds serenity to their woodland habitat.

Spotting one may prove to be harder but listen out for their calls to help narrow where they might be in your area.

Specific Locations to Find the Swainson's Thrush In Tennessee

- **Great Smoky Mountains National Park:** Look for Swainson's Thrushes in the dense understory along trails such as the Alum Cave Trail and the Roaring Fork Motor Nature Trail, especially during migration and breeding seasons.

- **Radnor Lake State Park (Nashville)**: This park features wooded areas and riparian habitats that provide suitable nesting and foraging opportunities for Swainson's Thrushes.

- **Cherokee National Forest**: Explore the forest's mixed woodlands and riparian zones, where these thrushes are often found during migration and nesting.

- **Long Hunter State Park**: The park's wooded trails and shrub areas along J. Percy Priest Lake attract Swainson's Thrushes, especially in spring and fall.

- **Cumberland Gap National Historical Park**: The diverse habitats in the park, including dense forests and thickets, are ideal for spotting Swainson's Thrushes.

- **South Cumberland State Park**: Areas with dense vegetation and forest edges in this park provide good opportunities for observing these thrushes.

- **Local Parks and Nature Reserves**: Look for Swainson's Thrushes in parks with mature trees and dense underbrush, such as Percy Warner Park in Nashville and Shelby Farms Park in Memphis.

20. GREATER WHITE-FRONTED GOOSE

The Greater White-fronted Goose is an interesting waterfowl species that has a very distinctive look and also migrates. It's an average-sized goose that measures about 26 to 30 inches in length, with a typical white patch on the forehead, after which it's named. Its plumage is generally brown with mixed gray and black feathers; the pinkish-orange bill provides an exciting color contrast. Particularly in migration, the species often appears in large flocks and gives a busy scene in the skies.

Greater White-fronted Geese are essentially tundra breeders of western Alaska and northern Canada, making long migrations to more temperate climates for the winter months to central and southern United States, where they seek out farm fields and wetlands. These geese can be commonly observed in wetlands, rice fields, and open fields where they forage for grains, grasses, and aquatic plants. Being adapted to different habitats, they sometimes get very common during the migration period, therefore gathering hundreds.

One of the most engaging aspects of the Greater White-fronted Goose is its vocalization. They produce many different honking calls, which are fairly commonly heard in flight or when congregating in large gatherings. These sounds are lively additions to their assemblies during migration and serve to communicate among members of the flock. I love listening to the geese honk at our local parks!

Nesting is carried out on grasslands near water where the female lays a clutch of four to six eggs. The young goslings are precocial, able to leave the nest shortly after hatching and start foraging.

Specific Locations to Find the Greater White-Fronted Goose

- **Reelfoot Lake State Park:** This wetland area is a prime spot for various waterfowl, including Greater White-fronted Geese, especially during migration in late fall and early spring.

- **Hatchie National Wildlife Refuge**: Located along the Hatchie River, this refuge provides excellent habitat for migratory geese and other waterfowl.

- **Tennessee National Wildlife Refuge**: This refuge is known for attracting a variety of waterfowl, including Greater White-fronted Geese, particularly during their migration periods.

- **Pickwick Landing State Park**: Situated along the Tennessee River, this park offers opportunities to see migratory geese, especially in the winter months.

- **Lake Isom National Wildlife Refuge**: This refuge provides suitable habitat for waterfowl and is often visited by Greater White-fronted Geese during migration.

- **Local Agricultural Fields**: During migration, Greater White-fronted Geese often feed in open agricultural fields. Look for them in rice, corn, and soybean fields in regions like the Mississippi Alluvial Plain.

- **Shelby Farms Park (Memphis)**: This large park features lakes and open areas where migratory geese can often be seen during the winter months.

21. Wild Turkey

The wild turkey is a native North American bird that is highly regarded, both for its remarkable plumage and for great cultural importance. They can be found in hardwood forests, grasslands, and other habitats; very good examples of adaptability and toughness. I personally have never seen a wild turkey before but I would love to! They form part of an important ecological link by helping to disperse seeds and acting as prey for other animals, such as the fox and birds of prey.

Some of the main features that distinguish wild turkeys are that the toms are much larger in size than the females. They reflect iridescent feathers in colors of bronze, green, and copper. One of their striking features is that when spread out, their fan-shaped tail reaches an extraordinary length that exceeds over four feet. They have a fleshy wattle and snood attached, which changes color with one's mood-always changing when courting.

The social aspects of wild turkeys relate to the fact that they are highly intelligent with complex behaviors. Especially because they have been known to flock in certain months of the year such as winter and in those systems, they can establish a social hierarchy. Their capability to communicate is fine-tuned by using a variety of calls that warn about impending danger, locate members of their flock, and even win a mate. These vocalizations will be especially important for survival while developing a means for social bonding at the same time.

The wild turkey figures immensely in American history and cultural tradition. Well before the time of the European settlers, it was one of the staples of the indigenous people, then later also symbolic of Thanksgiving celebrations in the United States. Indeed, Benjamin Franklin once famously proposed the turkey as the national bird, because he felt it had native qualities superior to the bald eagle.

Specific Locations to Find the Wild Turkey in Tennessee

- **Great Smoky Mountains National Park:** This expansive park offers diverse habitats, from hardwood forests to meadows, making it a prime location for spotting wild turkeys.

- **Land Between the Lakes National Recreation Area**: This area features a mix of forests and open land, providing ideal conditions for wild turkeys.

- **Cumberland Gap National Historical Park**: The park's varied terrain and abundant wildlife make it a good spot for observing wild turkeys.

- **Cherokee National Forest**: With its vast forests and mountainous regions, this area supports a healthy population of wild turkeys.

- **State Wildlife Management Areas (WMAs)**: Several WMAs, like the **Hatchie River WMA** and **Bledsoe Creek WMA**, are known for their wild turkey populations and provide excellent hunting and observation opportunities.

- **Local Parks and Greenways**: Many city parks and greenways across Tennessee, such as **Shelby Farms Park** in Memphis, also have populations of wild turkeys.

22. GOLDEN EAGLE

Golden Eagles are among those commanding birds of prey, celebrated for their enormity, elegance in the air, and hunting capability. Populations exist in most parts of the Northern Hemisphere and in high concentrations in mountainous areas; they are considered emblems of strength and freedom. Reaching up to seven feet on a wingspan, the golden eagle can fly magnificently, attaining altitudes at very high levels while scanning for prey. They are beautiful to watch soaring through the air.

These golden eagles have dark brown plumage, usually with gold highlights on the back of their heads and necks. With great eyesight, they can spot their prey miles away and are formidable hunters. Their diet generally consists of small to medium-sized mammals, such as rabbits, hares, and rodents, though birds are taken where needed. This is often accompanied by its hunting strategy of gliding high over its territory and plunging down with incredible speed in order to surprise its prey.

Socially, golden eagles are generally considered solitary or in pairs, particularly during the breeding season. They nest on cliffs or tall trees in huge nests called eyries, which they visit year after year. One to four eggs are laid by the female with incubation and childcare being the domain of both parents. The eaglets fledge after about three months, but they may remain dependent on the parents for another three to six months as they take their time learning to hunt and negotiate their environment.

Speaking culturally, golden eagles hold a great deal of symbolic meaning across different cultures, in which power, courage, and nobility are some of the common meanings derived from them. For this reason, in the United States, it has been under federal protection through the Bald and Golden Eagle Protection Act, underlining its protection as an act of conservation importance. Being at the top of the food chain means a golden eagle plays a crucial role in imposing ecological balance; hence, its preservation is quite vital for the health of the ecosystems. Elegant and powerful, it continues to amaze and leave people speechless, thus standing respected as an icon within the wildlife world.

Specific Locations to Find the Golden Eagle in Tennessee

- **Great Smoky Mountains National Park:** The park's high elevations and diverse habitats make it a suitable area for golden eagles, especially in winter when they migrate south.

- **Cherokee National Forest**: This forest features rugged terrain and open areas that attract golden eagles, particularly during migration.

- **Cumberland Gap National Historical Park**: The park's mountainous landscape provides excellent opportunities for observing golden eagles, especially during their migration periods in the fall and spring.

- **Lookout Mountain**: Near Chattanooga, this area is known for its scenic views and is a good spot to see golden eagles soaring overhead.

- **Wilderness Road State Park**: Located near the Kentucky border, this park offers habitat conducive to golden eagles, especially during migration.

- **State Wildlife Management Areas (WMAs)**: Several WMAs, such as the **Hatchie River WMA** and **Bridgestone/Firestone WMA**, are known to have golden eagles, particularly during winter.

23. SANDHILL CRANE

The Sandhill Crane is a striking migratory bird, expressing much grace and performing intricate courtship rituals. At about three to four feet in height, the crane can easily be recognized by its long neck, long legs, and distinctive gray plumage that is sometimes almost silver when the light catches it right. The red crowns and bold black facial markings add to their distinctive traits, which make them a favorite among birdwatchers and nature enthusiasts.

The highly social Sandhill Crane is often seen at any time of year in great flocks and the population congregates even more during migration. The cranes forage for food in wetlands of many types, from marshes and fields to shallow lakes, using their long bills very proficiently to discover a diet of mainly grains, seeds, and small invertebrates. They are also known for their loud, clear calls, which can be heard at very great distances and play a much more important role in their social behavior.

Of all the interesting facts about Sandhill Cranes, perhaps their dramatic courtship rituals stand out the most. Mating pairs perform a series of dances together that include leaps, bowing, and wing-flapping, reinforcing the pair bond and creating a visual display. Monogamous birds normally mate for life, returning to the same nesting areas every year and rearing their young in the security of wetlands.

Migration is an extremely important part of the life cycle of the Sandhill Crane. In the fall, this species migrates thousands of miles from their breeding grounds in Canada and the northern United States to their wintering areas in the southern United States and Mexico; the journey is a remarkable feat of endurance, an attestation to their resilience and adaptability.

In certain parts of Tennessee, there are Sandhill Craine festivals where you can come to spot them during their migration as well.

Specific Locations to Find the Sandhill Crane in Tennessee

- **Hatchie National Wildlife Refuge:** Located in West Tennessee, this refuge is an important stopover point for sandhill cranes during migration. The wetlands and open fields provide excellent foraging opportunities.

- **Reelfoot Lake State Park**: This area in northwest Tennessee is known for its rich birdlife, including sandhill cranes. The lake and surrounding wetlands attract these cranes, especially during migration.

- **Tennessee National Wildlife Refuge**: Situated in the west, this refuge provides ample habitat for sandhill cranes. The shallow waters and marshes are ideal for foraging and nesting.

- **Land Between the Lakes National Recreation Area**: This area features diverse habitats, making it a suitable spot for spotting sandhill cranes, particularly during migration.

- **Cherokee Wildlife Management Area**: Located in East Tennessee, this area supports various wildlife, including sandhill cranes during migration periods.

- **Great Smoky Mountains National Park**: While more famous for other wildlife, certain areas of the park may occasionally see sandhill cranes, particularly during migration.

24. WHOOPING CRANE

The whooping crane is beyond question a royal bird with an amazing body to touch alongside an impressive height. It stands almost five feet tall and counts as one of the tallest birds in North America, characterized by long legs, slender necks, peculiar white plumage, and a red crown on the head. It got its name from the loud hooping calls that may be heard from long distances, echoing across wetlands and grasslands. Once you hear them, you won't be able to miss them again!

Historically, the whooping crane has been abundant throughout much of North America, from Canada well into Texas. However, by the mid-20th century, because of habitat destruction, hunting, and

73

human encroachment, the population had plunged to fewer than 20 individuals-well into being declared extinct. This dramatic decline thus promoted serious conservation efforts in terms of habitat restoration and breeding programs.

Even today, the whooping crane is considered the epitome of wildlife conservation success. From recent estimates, this number has grown to over 800 today, again thanks in great part to the efforts of organizations such as the U.S. Fish and Wildlife Service and a host of non-profits that have installed protective measures in place, including key habitats and migration routes.

Specific Locations to Find the Whooping Crane in Tennessee

- **Hatchie National Wildlife Refuge:** This refuge in West Tennessee provides crucial wetland habitats that can attract migrating whooping cranes during their spring and fall migrations.

- **Reelfoot Lake**: Located in the northwest corner of Tennessee, this lake is an important area for migratory birds. Whooping cranes may stop here during their journey.

- **Tennessee Wildlife Resources Agency (TWRA) Lands**: Various TWRA-managed areas, particularly those with wetlands and open fields, may serve as stopover sites for migrating cranes.

- **Lake Isom National Wildlife Refuge**: Situated near Reelfoot Lake, this refuge is another potential spot for observing whooping cranes during migration.

To maximize your chances of spotting whooping cranes, it's best to visit these areas during the spring (March to April) and fall (September to November) migration seasons.

25. Killdeer

One of the most recognizable shorebirds in North America, due to singular appearance and habits, the killdeer has brownish-tan upperparts and white belly, with two black bands across the chest, making it an imposing and strikingly memorable sight. Commonly, they occur in open habitats such as fields, gravelly areas, and water edges.

Perhaps one of the most distinctive features of the killdeer is their behavior, particularly in the nesting season. Most killdeers nest on the ground, in simple scrapes in gravel or dirt. If nest sites are threatened, an intriguing distraction display may be employed. When a predator approaches near the nest, the killdeer will play the injured bird by faking a broken-wing act with the intent of leading the predator away from the nest. It is the one kind of behavior that shows how birds, while fighting for their lives, learn to adapt to the environment. It just shows how intelligent these birds really are.

Killdeers are also known for their call-a loud, melodious "kill-deer," which is both a name and warning. It is loudly and frequently given, particularly during the breeding season, and is an important part of their communication and territorial displays.

Besides their interesting behaviors, killdeers contribute to their ecosystems both as predators and prey. In general, their diet includes insects, larvae, and other small invertebrates, which they help control.

Specific Locations to Find the Killdeer in Tennessee

- **Reelfoot Lake:** This expansive wetland area in northwest Tennessee is a prime location for observing killdeers, especially during migration.

- **Hatchie National Wildlife Refuge**: This refuge offers open fields and wetlands, making it an ideal habitat for killdeers. They can often be seen foraging in the grass or near water.

- **Shelby Farms Park**: Located in Memphis, this large park features diverse habitats, including open fields and lakes, where killdeers can frequently be spotted.

- **Land Between the Lakes National Recreation Area**: This area between Kentucky and Barkley Lakes provides various habitats suitable for killdeers, including shorelines and open fields.

- **Wetlands and Fields Near Agricultural Areas**: Killdeers are often found in rural areas, especially in fields and along the edges of agricultural lands, where they forage for insects.

- **Norris Dam State Park**: This park features open fields and areas near water, making it another good spot for observing killdeers.

To increase your chances of spotting killdeers, visit these locations during the spring and summer breeding season (April to July) or during migration in the spring and fall.

26. UPLAND SANDPIPER

The upland sandpiper is an odd shorebird because of the habitat preference and some remarkable behaviors that set them aside from most shorebirds. While most of its shorebird relatives are seen on coastal areas, the upland sandpiper normally frequents open grasslands, agricultural fields, and savannas throughout North America. The long-legged, slender-necked bird with strikingly patterned plumage in mixed brown and buff tones is truly characteristic of affording very excellent camouflage among the grasses. In my opinion, it's such a cute bird to see wandering around!

The Upland Sandpiper measures about 12 to 14 inches in length and has an easily recognizable, elongated body shape and a distinctive call-melodious, rising and falling notes. This is one of the most common sounds in the upland sandpiper's breeding ground through much of its breeding season, in courtship and territoriality. Males are particularly vocal, singing while doing their aerial flight displays in order to attract females and show their remarkable flying abilities.

Breeding usually takes place into late spring and early summer; the nests are built on the ground in well-drained locations covered with grass. The clutch size is four eggs, laid by the female, which incubates while the male guards the territory. Hatched chicks are precocial, quite mature and mobile to forage for food almost immediately.

Specific Locations to Find the Upland Sandpiper in Tennessee

- **Hatchie National Wildlife Refuge:** This refuge in West Tennessee features open fields and grasslands, making it an excellent habitat for upland sandpipers, especially during migration and nesting season.

- **Land Between the Lakes National Recreation Area**: This area offers a mix of grasslands and open spaces, providing suitable environments for upland sandpipers to forage and nest.

- **Bledsoe Creek State Park**: Located near Gallatin, this park includes open fields and agricultural areas that attract upland sandpipers, particularly in the spring and summer.

- **Cumberland Plateau**: Certain regions of the Cumberland Plateau, with their expansive grasslands and pastures, can be ideal for spotting these birds.

- **Agricultural Fields**: Throughout rural Tennessee, especially in areas with low vegetation and crops, upland sandpipers may often be seen foraging.

To increase your chances of spotting upland sandpipers, visit these locations during the late spring to early summer (April to July) when they are nesting and more active.

27. AMERICAN KESTREL

The American kestrel is the smallest falcon in North America and is recognized by its bright plumage and admirable hunting prowess. It measures roughly 9 to 12 inches in length. This is a sexually dimorphic bird of prey, with males having bright blue-gray on their heads and wings, while females are warm rufous-brown. During its breeding season, both sexes display a distinctive pattern of black spots running along their backs with a well-defined black line from the beak through to the eye.

It is highly adaptable; the American kestrel can normally be found in open fields, grasslands, and most urban areas. This bird is most commonly seen perched on telephone wires or posts, peering down toward the ground for prey to eat. They are gorgeous to see and hear when you get the chance. The diet consists mainly of small mammals, insects, and sometimes birds. Kestrels are a very gallant hunter; perhaps one of the most amazing skills of theirs is being able to stay mid-air, hovering while scanning below them for movement, a practice which sets these birds apart from other raptors.

Breeding usually takes place during spring when females lay 3 to 7 eggs in tree hollows or nest boxes provided by humans. Parents are known to be attentive to their young, feeding them a nutrient-rich diet that would keep them healthy and strong for their growth and development. The chicks fledge after about 30 days, ready to begin their journey into independence.

Specific Locations to Find the American Kestrel in Tennessee

- **Hatchie National Wildlife Refuge:** This refuge provides a mix of grasslands and wetlands, making it an excellent habitat for American kestrels.

- **Land Between the Lakes National Recreation Area**: This area features open fields and wooded edges, ideal for observing kestrels as they hunt for small mammals and insects.

- **Shelby Farms Park**: Located in Memphis, this large park has open fields and wetlands where kestrels are often seen perched on posts or hovering above the ground.

- **Cumberland Plateau**: The open fields and pastures in this region can attract American kestrels, especially during the breeding season.

- **Agricultural Areas**: Kestrels are frequently spotted in rural areas, particularly in agricultural fields where they can hunt for rodents and insects.

- **Great Smoky Mountains National Park**: While primarily known for its forests, the park has open areas and meadows that can attract kestrels, especially at lower elevations.

28. EASTERN KINGBIRD

The eastern kingbird is indeed a catchy songbird that boasts a fearless bearing and striking appearance. About 7 to 9 inches in length, this bird covers its whole head with a black cap, while the whole upperparts are gray, and the undersides are white. Furthermore, there is the not-so-subtle white tip on its tail. The eastern kingbird is usually seen perched on wires or high branches, and this bird is easily recognized by its sleek coloration due to its sharp contrasting colors and energetic dispositions. This is one of the easier birds to identify from above because of their contrasting colors.

The eastern kingbird is a somewhat adaptable species found within a range of habitats, generally inhabiting open areas like fields, pastures, and along the edges of forests. They are territorial during breeding and show aggressive displays around their nests to deter intruders. Their diet mostly consists of insects, although they have been recorded catching small birds and feeding on berries-an example of adaptability in predation.

The eastern kingbird migrates, wintering in Central and South America, and returning to North America in the spring. Their arrival is a welcome sign of warmer weather, and they are often seen in flocks during migration. Breeding usually takes place from late spring into early summer, with females laying a clutch of 3-6 eggs in a concealed nest built in shrubs or low trees. Both parents take part in raising the young and teaching them the ways of survival.

Specific Locations to Find the Eastern Kingbird in Tennessee

- **Hatchie National Wildlife Refuge:** This refuge features open fields and wetlands, providing ideal hunting and nesting grounds for eastern kingbirds.

- **Land Between the Lakes National Recreation Area**: The diverse habitats here, including fields and woodlands, attract eastern kingbirds, especially during migration and nesting.

- **Shelby Farms Park**: Located in Memphis, this large park has open areas and wetlands where eastern kingbirds can often be seen perched on wires or trees.

- **Cumberland Plateau**: Open pastures and fields in this region are good spots to observe these birds, particularly in the late spring and summer.

- **Agricultural Areas**: Rural farmlands and fields throughout Tennessee can be excellent places to find eastern kingbirds hunting for insects.

- **Great Smoky Mountains National Park**: While primarily forested, certain open areas and meadows within the park can attract eastern kingbirds, especially at lower elevations.

29. BARN SWALLOW

Its iridescent blue upperparts and forked tail are symptoms of its gracefulness and agility. This little passerine, about 6.5 to 7.5 inches in length, is seen flying over most of North America and indeed most of the world outside rural and agricultural areas. Barn Swallows grace the air with their elegant flight as they swoop and dive in pursuit of insects with wonderful acrobatics.

Barn swallows are highly social birds and sometimes nest in colonies. They like to construct their nests from mud in protected locations, such as under eaves, within barns, or on the sides of buildings, for which they derive their name. If you have a barn nearby, that's a safe place to try and find them! The nest is a structure of mud and grass, intricately molded to hold their eggs safely. Females typically lay between three to seven eggs, of which incubation is done by both parents. After hatching, the chicks grow rapidly and are capable of flying within two to three weeks.

These birds have an eminently insectivorous diet, most of it being made up of flies, mosquitoes, and other small insects caught on the wing. Their foraging strategy consists of skimming low over water or open fields, showcasing their remarkable aerial agility. Barn swallows are also attributed with long migrations, flying thousands of miles between their North American breeding grounds and wintering habitats in Central and South America.

Specific Locations to Find the Barn Swallow in Tennessee

- **Agricultural Fields:** Barn swallows thrive in farming regions, often seen flying over fields and pastures as they hunt for insects.

- **Hatchie National Wildlife Refuge**: This refuge features open areas and wetlands that attract barn swallows, especially during the breeding season.

- **Shelby Farms Park**: Located in Memphis, this large park has open fields and lakes where barn swallows can be observed foraging for insects.

- **Land Between the Lakes National Recreation Area**: This area offers diverse habitats, including open fields and water bodies, ideal for barn swallow sightings.

- **Cumberland Plateau**: The open pastures and fields in this region provide excellent foraging opportunities for barn swallows during the warmer months.

30. YELLOW WARBLER

One of the most easily recognized songbirds, the yellow warbler is bright and cheery, with its bright yellow plumage accented by a melodic song. About 4.5 to 5.5 inches in length, the male yellow warbler is particularly striking, given his golden-yellow body against an olive-green back. The females and young birds share the same basic coloration but will more often have brown streaks across the chest, giving them a much more subdued appearance. Listening to their song is a beautiful treat for birdwatchers.

The habitats of yellow warblers are varied and range from riparian zones, wetlands to shrubby areas. They are abundant during the breeding season in North America, thriving in thick vegetation near water. Because of these preferences, they are integral to any ecosystem's functioning and diet, helping control insect populations with diets composed mainly of insects and spiders.

These birds are often characterized by sweet, warbling songs, which provide them with territorial establishment and allure of mates. Breeding usually takes place from late spring to early summer with females building cup-shaped nests in shrubs or low trees. They have about four to six eggs, which both parents help incubate and care for after hatching. The young fledge within two weeks, soon becoming independent.

During migration, yellow warblers migrate over long distances, wintering in Central America and parts of South America. Their migratory habits also make them adaptable, as they may be found in a wide variety of habitats over their range.

Specific Locations to Find the Yellow Warbler in Tennessee

- **Hatchie National Wildlife Refuge:** This refuge features wetlands and riparian areas that provide ideal nesting habitats for yellow warblers, especially during the spring and summer.

- **Land Between the Lakes National Recreation Area**: With its diverse ecosystems, including forests and wetlands, this area is a great spot for observing yellow warblers during migration and nesting.

- **Reelfoot Lake**: This natural lake in northwest Tennessee has extensive marshlands and dense vegetation, making it a prime location for yellow warblers.

- **Great Smoky Mountains National Park**: Various locations within the park, particularly along streams and in lower elevation areas, can host yellow warblers during their breeding season.

- **Shelby Farms Park**: This large park in Memphis features open fields, wetlands, and wooded areas where yellow warblers are often spotted.

31. INDIGO BUNTING

The indigo bunting is one of the most exquisitely fine birds, with an eye-catching brilliant blue plumage and its melodious song. It is always spectacular during its breeding season when it appears quite dramatically in brilliant, cobalt blue against the blackness of wings and tail, while females reflect brown and streaked feathers perfect for giving them camouflage in their habitats. This dimorphism makes the indigo bunting an interesting species to observe. Their color is actually so bright that it's an amazing feat to see one. The first one I saw one in my yard, I couldn't believe it.

Indigo buntings utilize everything from open woodlands to shrubby and field-edge habitats, ranging across North America. This bird species is common throughout most of the eastern and central United States during the breeding season, while in winter, it migrates as far as southern Mexico and Central America. Its normal preference is for brushy, shrubby habitats, so that they could be fairly common sights in rural settings or along road cuts.

These birds are known for their beautiful songs, almost like flute music, which they use to attract mates and defend their territory. Males do most of their singing from conspicuous perches and appear bright before the females. Breeding ranges from late spring into early summer; the female constructs a nest low in a shrub or grass, laying about three to five eggs, which she then incubates for two weeks. The chicks, once hatched, are brooded by both parents and fed a diet rich in insects and seeds.

Specific Locations to Find the Indigo Bunting in Tennessee

- **Hatchie National Wildlife Refuge:** This refuge offers open fields and brushy areas that provide excellent habitat for indigo buntings during the spring and summer.

- **Land Between the Lakes National Recreation Area**: With its mix of forests, fields, and wetlands, this area is a great place to observe indigo buntings, particularly near shrubby edges.

- **Great Smoky Mountains National Park**: Various locations within the park, especially at lower elevations and along forest edges, can host indigo buntings during the breeding season.

- **Shelby Farms Park**: Located in Memphis, this park features open fields and wooded areas where indigo buntings can often be seen and heard singing.

- **Cumberland Plateau**: The open fields and pastures in this region are good habitats for indigo buntings, particularly in spring and early summer.

32. PAINTED BUNTING

The painted bunting is one of North America's most colorfully painted birds, celebrated for its brightly colored plumage and pleasing demeanor. Males are especially striking, sporting bright blue wings and head, a green back, and a deep red belly. Females, while not as flashy, are no less handsome in their warm yellows and olive tones, which go far to help them better blend into the surrounding environment. I have always loved them and hope to see one in the wild one day.

The painted bunting is a bird of the southeastern United States during the breeding season, ranging to central Texas, Louisiana, and Florida. Present in open woodlands, shrub lands, and fields especially near water. It's a very migratory species with wintering populations in Central America into southern Mexico.

In the breeding season, male painted buntings are similarly vocal, singing melodic songs to attract females and establish territory. Nesting ranges from late spring into early summer, where the female constructs a cup-shaped nest out of dense vegetation, lays three to five eggs, and incubates them for approximately 12 days. Both parents feed the chicks, which fledge approximately 10-12 days after hatching.

Specific Locations to Find the Painted Bunting in Tennessee

- **Reelfoot Lake:** This area in northwest Tennessee has a mix of wetlands and shrubbery, making it a suitable habitat for painted buntings during migration and breeding.

- **Hatchie National Wildlife Refuge**: This refuge offers diverse habitats, including open fields and brushy areas, ideal for observing painted buntings, especially in late spring and summer.

- **Land Between the Lakes National Recreation Area**: With its variety of habitats, including forest edges and meadows, this area is a great place to find painted buntings during their nesting season.

- **Shelby Farms Park**: Located in Memphis, this large park features open spaces and dense shrubs where painted buntings can often be seen, particularly in migration seasons.

- **Great Smoky Mountains National Park**: While primarily forested, certain lower-elevation areas and clearings can attract painted buntings during the breeding season.

33. WESTERN MEADOWLARK

The western meadowlark is one of the most striking songbirds in its appearance, commonly recognized by its yellow belly and sanguine call. It is about 7 to 9 inches in length, with a bright yellow underpart, a black "V" on its chest, and brown-streaked upperparts that afford the bird excellent camouflage in its usual habitats of grasslands. In all, the western meadowlark is distributed throughout the western United States, Canada, and into much of Mexico, occurring in open fields, prairies, and grasslands. With so many open fields throughout Tennessee's farmland, they are a great bird to spot.

One of the most distinctive features of the western meadowlark is their song, a rich, flute-like melody. This call attracts a mate, establishes territory, and communicates between the meadowlarks. The song is quintessential in American prairies; during the breeding period, the males are noted for making a series of songs from conspicuous perches like fence posts or tall grasses.

Breeding typically occurs from late spring through summer. Females build nests on the ground, concealed in grasses, where they lay three to six eggs. The chicks are precocial, meaning that they are relatively mature at hatching and able to leave the nest shortly thereafter; however, they depend on their parents for food for several weeks.

Being ground foragers, the main diet of the western meadowlark consists of a consumption of insects, seeds, and grasses.

Specific Locations to Find the Western Meadowlark in Tennessee

- **Hatchie National Wildlife Refuge:** This refuge features open fields and grasslands, providing ideal habitats for western meadowlarks, especially during the spring and summer.

- **Reelfoot Lake**: The surrounding agricultural fields and wetlands can attract western meadowlarks, particularly during migration and nesting seasons.

- **Land Between the Lakes National Recreation Area**: With its diverse habitats, including fields and pastures, this area is a good spot for observing these birds.

- **Cumberland Plateau**: The open grasslands and fields in this region provide suitable environments for western meadowlarks.

34. RED-WINGED BLACKBIRD

The red-winged blackbird is a fantastically beautiful and familiar bird throughout most of North America. The species can easily be identified by its shiny black plumage with the striking red and yellow wing patches of the male, generally to be found in wetlands, marshes, and grassy areas. The females are pretty soberly colored with streaky brown plumage, affording them maximum camouflage among the densely packed vegetation. I actually spotted one on the outskirts of town once!

The red-winged blackbirds are extremely social and, therefore, usually found in flocks, especially while migrating. Their loud, distinctive calls, which sound like a sharp "conk-la-ree," characterize the wetland environments in which they occur, given their fiercely defensive nature regarding territory. Males establish and guard territories in spring, using their vocalizations to deter rivals and attract mates. The breeding usually begins during late March and extends into the summer when females build nests in dense vegetation close to water. Typically, three to six eggs are laid and incubation duties are shared between the two parents.

The members of this family are essentially omnivorous; they eat almost anything, including seeds, grains, and insects. During the time when it breeds, the presence of insects becomes essential in order to provide protein to the growing chicks. Their adaptability to different types of habitat-mostly agricultural fields and even urban areas-contributes much to their wide presence.

Specific Locations to Find the Red-Winged Blackbird in Tennessee

- **Hatchie National Wildlife Refuge:** This refuge features wetlands, marshes, and grasslands that provide ideal habitats for red-winged blackbirds, especially during the breeding season.

- **Reelfoot Lake**: The lake's surrounding marshy areas and fields are great for observing red-winged blackbirds, particularly during migration and nesting.

- **Land Between the Lakes National Recreation Area**: This area offers a mix of wetlands and open fields, making it a good spot for red-winged blackbirds.

- **Great Smoky Mountains National Park**: While primarily known for its forests, certain wetland areas and meadows within the park can attract these birds.

- **Shelby Farms Park**: Located in Memphis, this large park has a variety of habitats, including wetlands and open fields, where red-winged blackbirds can often be seen.

WATER BIRDS OF TENNESSEE

35. BLACK BELLIED WHISTLING DUCK

The black-bellied whistling duck is an interesting waterfowl species, known by its remarkable aspect and unique vocalizations. It measures about 20 to 24 inches in length. This duck has a shining brown body, striking black belly, and a long neck tapered at the end. Its most distinctive characteristics are the bright orange bill and striking pinkish legs. Unlike many other ducks, black-bellied whistling ducks have more upright postures; hence, they look rather graceful while foraging or wading in shallow waters. They are very cute ducks to watch swimming too!

Native to both Central and South America, the range of the black-bellied whistling duck has extended to include the southern parts of the United States, with areas like Texas and Louisiana being some of its key locations. They like to stay in wetlands, ponds, rice fields, and other areas where food is plenty and nesting sites are appropriate. They primarily feed on seeds, grains, and aquatic plants. Most of them are quite famous for their foraging behavior, dwelling in fields or along the edges of various water bodies.

One of the most interesting things about black-bellied whistling ducks is their call. They get their names from their strange, whistled calls, which are heard from great numbers of birds. These are social birds that often travel in large flocks, mainly during migration and non-breeding periods.

Breeding typically occurs during late spring throughout summer. Females construct their nests on the ground in tall grass or dense vegetation near water. They lay around 8 to 12 eggs, which both parents incubate and defend.

Specific Locations to Find the Black Bellied Whistling Duck in Tennessee

- **Hatchie National Wildlife Refuge:** This refuge features wetlands and open water areas that attract black-bellied whistling ducks, particularly in spring and fall.

- **Reelfoot Lake**: The lake's marshy edges and diverse aquatic habitats provide excellent opportunities for observing these ducks.

- **Land Between the Lakes National Recreation Area**: With its mix of lakes, wetlands, and fields, this area can be a good spot for finding black-bellied whistling ducks.

Great Smoky Mountains National Park: While primarily forested, certain wetland areas within the park may host these ducks during migration.

36. MUTE SWAN

It is among the most familiar and iconic waterfowl species, with much admiration for its elegant, gracious appearance while swimming. The white plumage, elongated neck, and its peculiar curvature give the mute swan a length of about 50 to 60 inches, ranking it as one of the biggest swan species. A bright orange bill adorns the mute swans as adults and is quite striking; there is also a prominent black knob at its base that adds to their elegance. Mute swans are absolutely gorgeous and I love being able to spot one in the water.

Native to Europe and Asia, mute swans were brought to North America in the 19th century and since then have established populations across the continent. In large part, they inhabit ponds, lakes, and slow rivers, with a preference for sites with considerable vegetation for feeding on aquatic plants, seeds, and small invertebrates. Mute swans form strong pair bonds; many pairs persist throughout many consecutive years, or for life. They are cavity-nesting birds; during breeding, the birds build large nests of reeds and grasses on or near the water surface where the female lays a clutch of cygnets-four to seven eggs on average.

Specific Locations to Find the Mute Swan in Tennessee

- **Shelby Farms Park:** Located in Memphis, this large park features lakes and wetlands where mute swans are often seen swimming.

- **Reelfoot Lake:** This natural lake in northwest Tennessee has marshy edges and open water, providing suitable habitat for mute swans.

- **Hatchie National Wildlife Refuge:** This refuge includes wetlands and ponds, which can attract mute swans, especially during migration seasons.

- **Chickamauga Lake:** The expansive waters of this lake near Chattanooga provide habitat for various waterfowl, including mute swans.

- **Local Parks and Ponds:** Many urban parks with ponds or lakes may host mute swans, particularly in larger cities like Nashville and Knoxville.

37. MUSCOVY DUCK

The Muscovy duck is probably one of the most odd waterfowl in Central and South America, increasingly colonizing the southern United States. It can be identified by its peculiar appearance, sexual dimorphism in size with the males being larger and the distinctive green and black plumage, with iridescent highlights, while females are much duller, often brown and mottled. Perhaps the most characteristic feature of the Muscovy duck is its red facial caruncles- or fleshy growths. These enlarge in males and give them a rather bizarre yet almost humorous look. I personally love them because they are so endearing!

These are adaptable birds of wetlands, lakes, and urban areas. They are often seen foraging for food in parks and gardens, where they consume a wide diet of seeds, grains, fruits, and insects. Unlike most of the other duck species, Muscovy ducks are powerful fliers, and roosting in trees can be observed to satisfy the adaptation in various environmental conditions.

The most characteristic features of these ducks are the specific vocalizations, which lie within the range from soft coos to loud hisses. During the nesting season, males exhibit displays and take territories, females build nests on or near the ground in tree cavities, laying 8 to 16 eggs.

Specific Locations to Find the Muscovy Duck in Tennessee

- **Shelby Farms Park:** Located in Memphis, this large park features lakes and wetlands where Muscovy ducks are often seen foraging and swimming.

- **Reelfoot Lake**: This natural lake in northwest Tennessee has diverse habitats, including marshes and open water, which can attract Muscovy ducks, particularly in warmer months.

- **Local Parks and Gardens**: Many urban parks across cities like Nashville, Knoxville, and Chattanooga may host Muscovy ducks, especially those with ponds or lakes.

- **Riverfront Parks**: Areas along rivers, such as the Cumberland River in Nashville, often attract a variety of waterfowl, including Muscovy ducks.

- **Agricultural Areas**: Farms with ponds or water features may also provide habitat for Muscovy ducks, especially in rural settings.

- **Great Smoky Mountains National Park**: While less common, certain water bodies in the park may occasionally attract Muscovy ducks, particularly in developed areas.

38. AMERICAN WIGEON

The American wigeon is one of the most striking and adaptable dabbling ducks native to North America. The male American wigeon has a bright greenish-colored head with a white crown and a chestnut-colored breast, while females are more subdued, featuring mottled brown plumage with a lighter-colored face. The length of an adult male is about 19 to 23 inches long and may easily be recognized by its whistling calls. They camouflage very well in fields so try listening for their calls if you can't seem to find them.

While breeding, American wigeons are normally found on freshwater wetlands, marshes, and ponds throughout northern parts of the United States and Canada. However, during winter, they migrate to southern coastal areas and estuaries, where large flocks are commonly present. It is this potential flexibility in habitat use that makes it an integral part of rural and urban surroundings.

As highly herbivorous, they feed on aquatic plants, grass, and grains. These ducks have been made famous by their foraging behavior in taking food by grazing on land and dabbling at the water's surface. It is due to this aspect of dieting versatility that they are able to survive in different ecological niches, from marshes to agricultural fields.

They breed from late spring to early summer where females construct nests in dense vegetation near water. Females lay a clutch of 6 to 10 eggs, which they incubate for about 25 days. Young are precocial, leaving the nest shortly after hatching and joining their mother in foraging for food.

Specific Locations to Find the American Wigeon in Tennessee

- **Hatchie National Wildlife Refuge:** This refuge features marshes and wetlands that attract American wigeons, particularly in the fall and winter.

- **Reelfoot Lake**: Known for its diverse bird life, Reelfoot Lake is a great spot for observing American wigeons, especially during migration.

- **Lake Chickamauga**: This lake in southeast Tennessee provides suitable habitat for waterfowl, including American wigeons, during the winter months.

- **Pickwick Landing State Park**: The park's lakes and wetlands attract a variety of waterfowl, including American wigeons, particularly in the colder months.

- **Shelby Farms Park**: Located in Memphis, this large park features ponds and wetlands where American wigeons can often be seen.

39. NORTHERN SHOVELER

The Northern Shoveler is a very distinctive and easily recognizable dabbling duck because of its peculiar appearance and interesting behavior. The males are brightly colored: the head is an iridescent green, the chest is white, and the sides are chestnut-colored. The most striking feature of the northern shovelers, however, is their exceptionally big, spatula-shaped bill, distinctive from all other ducks. The females are much more subtle; mottled brown to facilitate furtive nesting. These are such fun and cute ducks to spot, especially because of their bills.

In the breeding season, which generally runs from late winter into early summer, northern shovelers can be found in freshwater wetlands, marshes, and ponds throughout North America. They prefer a habitat with dense aquatic vegetation owing to the availability of their principal foodstuffs, such as plant matter, seeds, and small invertebrates. The unique bill structure allows this species to efficiently filter food from the water, scooping both plant material and small organisms.

During migration, the Northern Shovelers can be seen in large flocks; sometimes, these are mixed with other waterbirds. The social behaviors include a characteristic courtship display, where males make spectacular maneuvers, thus showing themselves off in colorful plumage and bills to attract females.

Breeding typically occurs in northern parts of the United States and Canada. Females construct nests on the ground in tall grasses and reeds, laying a clutch of 8 to 12 eggs. The chicks are precocial, leaving the nest shortly after hatching and foraging for food with their mother.

Specific Locations to Find the Northern Shoveler in Tennessee

- **Hatchie National Wildlife Refuge:** This refuge features wetlands and marshes that are excellent for spotting northern shovelers, especially during fall and winter.

- **Reelfoot Lake**: Known for its diverse birdlife, Reelfoot Lake attracts many waterfowl, including northern shovelers, particularly during migration periods.

- **Lake Chickamauga**: This reservoir in southeast Tennessee provides suitable habitat for various waterfowl, including northern shovelers, during the winter months.

- **Pickwick Landing State Park**: The park's lakes and wetlands can host northern shovelers, especially in colder seasons when waterfowl are more prevalent.

- **Shelby Farms Park**: Located in Memphis, this large park has ponds and marshy areas that often attract northern shovelers during migration.

40. BUFFLEHEAD

The bufflehead is a small but striking diving duck and is known for its unique appearance and lively demeanor. About 12 to 16 inches in length, the male bufflehead is especially striking with his glossy black head bearing a large iridescent white patch extending from the eye back toward the rear of the head. Mainly white with black wings, it's easy to spot both flying and on the water. The female is much more subdued in color but just as charming, with a brownish body and a white cheek patch. They truly are adorable ducks especially with the little pouf on their head.

The buffleheads are essentially from North America and migrate to the marine and freshwater habitats during winter periods. They favor places like lakes, ponds, and estuary places when diving for their food. Their food is comprised of small fish, invertebrates, and water plants. Their reputation is that of agile divers that plunge with quickness and stay beneath the water surface for as long as 30 seconds while in search of food.

They usually breed in the north, including Canada and northern parts of the United States. During their breeding season, females lay a clutch of eggs in tree cavities or abandoned woodpecker holes near water, laying between approximately 5 to 10 eggs. Females alone incubate the eggs, while the ducklings are precocial, leaving the nest shortly after they hatch to join their mother.

Specific Locations to Find the Bufflehead in Tennessee

- **Hatchie National Wildlife Refuge:** This refuge offers a variety of wetlands and ponds, making it a good place to see buffleheads, particularly during the winter months.

- **Reelfoot Lake**: Known for its diverse bird populations, Reelfoot Lake is a prime spot for observing buffleheads during migration and winter.

- **Chickamauga Lake**: This reservoir in southeastern Tennessee provides suitable habitat for buffleheads, especially during the colder months.

- **Pickwick Landing State Park**: The park's lakes and surrounding wetlands often attract buffleheads and other waterfowl during winter.

- **Shelby Farms Park**: Located in Memphis, this large park features ponds and marshy areas where buffleheads can frequently be observed.

41. COMMON LOON

The common loon is a striking aquatic bird famous for its haunting calls and remarkable diving abilities. Characterized by a sharp, pointed bill and streamlined body, the common loon primarily lives in northern regions of North America, which include Canada and parts of the northern United States. Adults can reach lengths of about 28 to 30 inches and have a wingspan of approximately 50 to 60 inches. During the breeding season, males and females acquire striking black-and-white checkered plumage that is excellent camouflage against the surface of the water.

The common loon is a very accomplished diver, with a depth limit of as much as 200 feet in its search for fish and invertebrates, its staple foods. Webbed feet enable them to be swift swimmers, but on land they appear to be rather clumsy. They nest on lonely lakes, laying one to three eggs on a shallow scrape on the shore. These nests may often be concealed in thick vegetation to protect them from predators.

One of the most fascinating things about the common loon is the hauntingly beautiful call that echoes across northern lakes for a variety of purposes, including communicating with its mate and signaling territory. Their calls are an iconic sound in the northern wilds. I love listening to their calls because there is no other call like it.

Specific Locations to Find the Common Loon in Tennessee

- **Reelfoot Lake:** This natural lake in northwest Tennessee is known for diverse bird populations, including common loons, particularly during migration in spring and fall.

- **Chickamauga Lake**: Located near Chattanooga, this large reservoir can attract common loons, especially during winter months when they may be seen resting or foraging.

- **Kentucky Lake**: The expansive waters of Kentucky Lake, along the Tennessee-Kentucky border, can host common loons during migration.

- **Norris Lake**: This large reservoir in eastern Tennessee provides suitable habitat for common loons during their migratory journeys.

42. COMMON MERGANSER

The common merganser is an exceedingly handsome duck, having an undulated body with a sharp bill and remarkable diving skills. The mergansers are placed in the family Anatidae, wherein all members have their necks rather long, with a pointed bill and with unique plumage. An adult male is wholly stunningly attractive, with its head glossy green, body white, and back black; whereas females are very subdued, with a rusty red head, grayish-colored body. They both share the distinctive feature of a long bill fitted for catching fish, their main diet. Their bill is a helpful way to identify them in the wild as well.

Common mergansers are primarily found in freshwater lakes, rivers, and reservoirs, mainly during the breeding season in North America. They prefer clear and cold water with plenty of fish and can skillfully dive down in pursuit of them by using their keen eyesight to locate fish beneath the water surface. In fact, mergansers are very efficient swimmers, often diving to depths of 15 to 20 feet while foraging.

They usually breed in forested areas, mostly near water bodies; females build nests in tree cavities or beneath the roots and logs. Females lay a clutch of 6 to 12 eggs, which they incubate for approximately 30 days. The hatchlings are precocial, meaning that in a short period, they leave the nest and follow their mother to water, where they begin feeding themselves.

Specific Locations to Find the Common Merganser in Tennessee

- **Norris Lake:** This large reservoir in eastern Tennessee provides suitable habitat for common mergansers, especially during the winter months when they may be foraging for fish.

- **Chickamauga Lake**: Located near Chattanooga, this lake often attracts migrating common mergansers, particularly in the colder months.

- **Reelfoot Lake**: Known for its rich birdlife, Reelfoot Lake is a good spot for observing common mergansers during migration.

- **Kentucky Lake**: This expansive reservoir along the Tennessee-Kentucky border can host common mergansers during their migratory journeys.

43. PIED BILLED GREBE

The Pied-billed Grebe is a small, distinctive waterbird found throughout North America. About 13 to 15 inches in length, this grebe can readily be identified by its stout body with short neck and peculiar chunky bill that essentially is white during the breeding season with a bold black band through the center. Outside the breeding season, the plumage reduces to a more lowly brown and gray tones, so it goes very undistinguished into its wetland surroundings. These are such cute little birds and they are fun to spot for beginners.

Pied-billed grebes can be found in several freshwater habitats: ponds, lakes, marshes, and rivers. Generally speaking, they prefer thick vegetation. They feed on small fish, invertebrates, and water plants; all these are grasped by their skillful dives. Pied-billed grebes are good swimmers, diving into the water, and under the surface, pursuing their prey.

Pied-billed grebes build a nest with aquatic vegetation that floats in the water during its breeding season, late spring to early summer. Both parents incubate a clutch of about 4 to 8 eggs. Chicks are precocial; thus, they can leave the nest promptly after birth and become independent enough to swim, with an opportunity to ride the parent's back for safety.

Among all the behaviors of a pied-billed grebe, the most interesting is the ability to sink into the water in order not to be seen by predators. If it feels threatened, it can submerge abruptly and quickly, leaving above the water surface only its eyes.

Specific Locations to Find the Pied Billed Grebe in Tennessee

- **Hatchie National Wildlife Refuge:** This refuge features wetlands and ponds that are ideal for observing pied-billed grebes, especially in the spring and summer.

- **Reelfoot Lake**: Known for its rich birdlife, Reelfoot Lake is a great spot to see pied-billed grebes, particularly during migration.

- **Chickamauga Lake**: This large reservoir near Chattanooga often attracts pied-billed grebes during the winter and migration periods.

- **Pickwick Landing State Park**: The park's lakes and wetlands can host pied-billed grebes, especially in spring and early summer.

44. AMERICAN WHITE PELICAN

The American white pelican stands out as a big and striking waterbird that extends natively across North America. Renowned for its impressive size, the outstanding features of this pelican include its incredibly large wing span and heavy body. This pelican measures over 9 feet in terms of wing span and measures about 50 to 65 inches in terms of body length, making it one of the largest birds in North America. Conspicuous plumage, basically white, is accented with black wing tips, visible clearly in flight. The American white pelican has a large, long bill yellow during the breeding season, with an inflated pouch used for catching fish. Normally when you think of pelicans, you think of the beach. But you can see them in so many places in landlocked Tennessee too.

These pelicans primarily inhabit freshwater lakes, rivers, and wetlands, subsisting on an almost fish-constituted diet. They generally follow cooperative foraging wherein many birds often operate together to herd schools of fish towards shallow waters for easy catch. Their foraging behaviors indicate their social nature, along with their adaptability to diverse habitats.

American White Pelicans are ground-nesting colonial breeders, a process that typically occurs during the spring and summer seasons. Nests include vegetation and are usually located on islands or shorelines that are difficult to access to help protect their young from predators. Females lay 2 to 4 eggs in a clutch; incubation is performed by both parents.

Migration is an important component of the American white pelican life cycle. They breed in the northern U.S. and Canada, migrating to spend the winter months at warmer coastal areas; parts of Texas and California are included in their range. This particular aspect of the migratory habit expresses their adaptability to changing environments.

Specific Locations to Find the American White Pelican in Tennessee

- **Reelfoot Lake:** This natural lake in northwest Tennessee is a prime spot for observing American white pelicans, especially during migration in the spring and fall.

- **Kentucky Lake**: The expansive waters of Kentucky Lake, which borders Tennessee and Kentucky, can attract American white pelicans during their migratory journeys.

- **Chickamauga Lake**: Located near Chattanooga, this large reservoir is another area where American white pelicans can be seen, particularly during winter.

- **Hatchie National Wildlife Refuge**: This refuge features wetlands and ponds that are ideal for waterfowl, including American white pelicans, especially during migration.

- **Pickwick Landing State Park**: The park's lakes and surrounding areas provide suitable habitat for spotting pelicans during migration.

- **Local Wetlands and Ponds**: Various wetlands and large ponds throughout Tennessee may host American white pelicans, particularly during migration and winter.

45. DOUBLE CRESTED CORMORANT

The double-crested cormorant is a very interesting waterbird with a number of unique features and ecological roles. Native to North America, it's characterized by a slender neck, hooked bill and plumage that is mainly black but has a shining aspect. The most striking feature of this bird is a double crest of feathers which develops during the breeding season, a factor that adds to its peculiar appearance. This feature can really help beginners identify them in the wild.

These cormorants are very adaptable, and one may find them living in various different aquatic regions, from lakes and rivers to even coasts. They are extremely capable divers and hunt their favored food of fish through propelling with their webbed feet in the water. Such predatory actions form an important constituent of the balance in aquatic ecosystems as it keeps fish populations under check. Because of this feeding behavior, they have, however, come into conflict with fisheries due to the great impact they have on the local fish stocks.

These double-crested cormorants are colonial nesters that build huge colonies, either in trees or on rocky shores. Their nesting behavior and social structures thus give a great deal of insight into avian behavior and ecology. They are also known for their odd drying ritual, where they spread their wings to dry themselves out after dives, sometimes making a striking silhouette against the water.

Specific Locations to Find the Double Crested Cormorant in Tennessee

- **Reelfoot Lake:** This large, shallow lake in the northwest part of the state is known for its diverse bird population, including double-crested cormorants.

- **Chickamauga Lake**: Located near Chattanooga, this reservoir offers ample fishing opportunities, attracting cormorants, especially in winter.

- **Percy Priest Lake**: Near Nashville, this lake is a popular spot for recreational activities and is often frequented by cormorants, particularly during migration.

- **Kentucky Lake**: Stretching along the Tennessee-Kentucky border, this expansive lake provides ideal habitat for cormorants, especially in the spring and fall.

- **Mississippi River**: The river serves as a migratory route for many bird species, including double-crested cormorants, making various spots along the river potential viewing locations.

- **Lakes and Rivers in State Parks**: Parks like **Fall Creek Falls State Park** and **Cumberland Mountain State Park** feature lakes and rivers where cormorants can often be seen.

46. GREAT BLUE HERON

The great blue heron is a noble bird widely admired for its stunning looks and ecological importance. Standing as tall as five feet with a wingspan of up to six and a half feet, it is the largest heron in North America. Its elongated neck and legs, together with the pointed bill, are well adapted for being a skillful predator in aquatic environments. These are gorgeous birds to watch as they walk through lakes with ease.

The habitat of the great blue heron includes different wetland systems, like lakes, rivers, marshes, and coastlines. Their diet consists mainly of fish, although they are opportunistic feeders and eat amphibians, small mammals, and invertebrates. Such food provides them with the ability to maintain a wide range of habitats, which helps keep ecological balances by regulating their prey.

The breeding season is common in spring, as these herons gather into colonies called rookeries. Nesting either in high trees or on the ground near water, they build enormous nests with a considerable amount of sticks and other vegetation. Females lay from three to seven eggs and incubation is by both parents. The chicks fledge in a couple of months, and family groups often hang around together for a little time after leaving the nest, learning important hunting skills from their parents.

Specific Locations to Find the Great Blue Heron in Tennessee

- **Reelfoot Lake:** This large, shallow lake in northwest Tennessee is a prime spot for observing great blue herons, especially during the breeding season.

- **Chickamauga Lake**: Located near Chattanooga, this reservoir provides ideal fishing grounds for herons, making it a good viewing area.

- **Percy Priest Lake**: Near Nashville, this lake features extensive shorelines and wetlands, attracting great blue herons throughout the year.

- **Cumberland River**: The river and its surrounding habitats are excellent for spotting herons, particularly in areas with shallow waters and abundant fish.

- **Great Smoky Mountains National Park**: Streams and rivers within the park, such as the Oconaluftee and Little Pigeon River, are potential spots to see great blue herons in a stunning natural setting.

- **Swan Creek Wildlife Management Area**: This area features wetlands and ponds, providing great opportunities for heron watching.

- **Nashville's Centennial Park**: The park's lake and surrounding areas can attract great blue herons, especially during migration periods.

- **Land Between the Lakes National Recreation Area**: This area offers diverse habitats, including lakes and wetlands, which are ideal for spotting herons.

47. CATTLE EGRET

The cattle egret is a very recognizable heron species that is well-known for its odd comportment and outstanding adaptability to new environments. Native originally to Africa and parts of Europe, this little white bird spread successfully over most of the world's regions, including North America, where it can be very commonly seen in agricultural areas. The cattle egrets are easily recognized by their white plumage, yellow bill, and generally short height of about 18-22 inches. They are very cute birds to watch and have a silly way about them that just makes you smile.

One of the most intriguing things about cattle egrets is their symbiotic relationship with large herbivores, particularly cattle. While these animals are grazing, the movement of grass and insects that may be below opens room for egrets to feed on such insects flushed out-like grasshoppers. This mutualistic interaction goes hand in hand for both species: the cattle get pest control, while the egrets obtain a food supply.

Highly adaptive to various habitats, cattle egrets range from wetlands to grasslands and even farmlands. Their colonies nest in trees or shrubs near water, constructing their nests during the breeding season where the males will show off their courtship rituals, puffing out their feathers, and doing an extravagant movement to attract females.

Specific Locations to Find the Cattle Egret in Tennessee

- **Reelfoot Lake:** This area features extensive wetlands and is a prime spot for observing a variety of bird species, including cattle egrets.

- **Hatchie National Wildlife Refuge**: Located near Brownsville, this refuge offers suitable wetland habitats where cattle egrets can often be seen foraging.

- **Land Between the Lakes National Recreation Area**: This region includes diverse habitats, including fields and wetlands, making it a great place for spotting these egrets.

- **Cumberland River**: Areas along the river, particularly near agricultural lands, provide ideal foraging opportunities for cattle egrets.

- **Local Farms and Pastures**: Cattle egrets are commonly seen in fields where livestock is present, as they often follow cattle to feed on insects.

- **Shelby Farms Park**: Located in Memphis, this large park has a variety of habitats, including wetlands and meadows, attracting cattle egrets.

- **Cheatham Wildlife Management Area**: This area offers a mix of wetlands and fields where cattle egrets can often be found foraging.

- **Tennessee River**: Various locations along the river, especially in agricultural zones, can be good for spotting these birds.

48. GLOSSY IBIS

The glossy ibis is an arresting waterbird due to its bizarre coloring and expressively flamboyant feeding manners. A medium-sized ibis, easily recognizable by its curving bill and its plumage, which reflects colors of deep browns, metallic greens, and purples, it adds grace to wetland habitats. Adults usually range from about 22 to 28 inches in length, with long legs and a long neck, for wading into shallow waters in search of food. Their long beak and gorgeous feathers can really help beginners identify them with ease.

Preferred wetland habitats of glossy ibises include marshes, estuaries, and rice fields. Their diet consists mainly of small fish, amphibians, insects, and crustaceans, which they probe for in muddy or shallow waters. This adaptability in feeding behavior contributes to their ecological function in the regulation of insect populations and maintenance of wetland ecosystem balance.

During breeding, the glossy ibises are known to be colony-forming nesters, often among reeds and grasses. Their nest is usually built with twigs and vegetation; there, the eggs will safely lie, often three or five, incubated by both parents until they become well looked-after young.

Specific Locations to Find the Glossy Ibis in Tennessee

- **Reelfoot Lake**: This large, shallow lake in northwest Tennessee is known for its rich birdlife and is a good place to observe glossy ibises, especially during migration.

- **Hatchie National Wildlife Refuge**: Located near Brownsville, this refuge features diverse wetland habitats that attract glossy ibises and other waterbirds.

- **Shelby Farms Park**: Situated in Memphis, this large park includes wetlands and ponds, making it a potential spot for seeing glossy ibises.

- **Cheatham Wildlife Management Area**: This area offers a mix of wetlands and open fields, providing suitable habitat for glossy ibises, particularly during migration.

- **Land Between the Lakes National Recreation Area**: With its varied habitats, including marshes and wetlands, this area is ideal for spotting glossy ibises.

- **Mississippi River**: Areas along the river, especially in agricultural regions, can be good for observing glossy ibises, particularly during their migration periods.

- **Tennessee National Wildlife Refuge**: Located along the Tennessee River, this refuge provides excellent habitats for various waterbirds, including glossy ibises.

49. WOOD STORK

The wood stork is one of the interesting types of wading birds native to wetlands of the southeastern United States, Central America, and northern South America. Recognized for its big size and striking look, the wood stork stands up to about 32-40 inches tall with a big wingspan of about 5.5 feet. Its plumage is white, with black wing tips and a black, unfeathered head that provides great contrast to its long, curved bill. This striking appearance makes the wood stork not only an impressively looking bird but also provides some very practical uses in its feeding behavior. This is a very interesting stork to watch as they wander around too.

The typical habitats of wood storks are freshwater and brackish wetlands, which include swamps, marshes, and river deltas. They are opportunistic feeders; their main foods usually consist of fish and crustaceans, taken using an interesting foraging behavior called "tactile foraging." While wading in shallow water, the sensitive bills feel for prey, snapping up quickly once they are detected. This foraging strategy identifies them as being adapted to a great variety of wetland environments.

During the breeding season, Wood Storks usually nest in trees or shrubs around water in colonies. The nests are platforms of sticks and are used year after year. A female typically lays 3 to 5 eggs and both parents share incubation duties and care for the chicks, showing great fidelity to the family.

Specific Locations to Find the Wood Stork in Tennessee

- **Reelfoot Lake:** This large, shallow lake in northwest Tennessee is an important habitat for various bird species, including wood storks, especially during migration.

- **Hatchie National Wildlife Refuge**: Located near Brownsville, this refuge features diverse wetlands that attract wood storks and other waterbirds.

- **Cheatham Wildlife Management Area**: This area includes wetlands and open fields, providing suitable habitat for wood storks, particularly during the warmer months.

- **Tennessee National Wildlife Refuge**: Situated along the Tennessee River, this refuge offers excellent wetland habitats for wood storks and other migratory birds.

- **Land Between the Lakes National Recreation Area**: With its mix of wetlands and forests, this area is a potential spot for observing wood storks.

- **Lakes and Marshes in State Parks**: Parks like **Cumberland Mountain State Park** and **Long Hunter State Park** have wetlands that may attract wood storks.

50. AMERICAN COOT

The American Coot is an interesting, generalized waterbird that is very common in each of North America's three major regions. Often confused with a duck, the coot is actually a member of the rail family and is known for its peculiarly shaped body, rounded head, and most especially its bright white bill, adorned by a prominent frontal shield. Adults coots are 12 to 16 inches long and are somberly colored to offset their brightly colored bill and red eyes. Their

They are really adaptive birds that might flourish in different aquatic environments, like freshwater lakes, marshes, and rivers. They also take omnivorous food that includes various water plants, seeds, insects, and crustaceans. Coots are capable swimmers and divers since their lobed feet propel them while catching food underwater.

American Coots are a medium-sized waterbird with a black head, neck, and belly; gray back, wings, and tail; and white bill and forehead. During breeding season-from spring through summer-American coots build floating nests of vegetation in shallow waters. Elaborate courtship displays include synchronized swimming and calling. A clutch usually consists of 8 to 12 eggs, and both parents incubate and raise the young. The young are precocial, swimming and foraging with their parents within days of hatching.

Specific Locations to Find the American Coot in Tennessee

- **Reelfoot Lake:** This large, shallow lake in northwest Tennessee is a prime habitat for American coots, especially during migration and breeding seasons.

- **Hatchie National Wildlife Refuge**: Located near Brownsville, this refuge features marshes and wetlands that attract coots and other waterbirds.

- **Tennessee National Wildlife Refuge**: Situated along the Tennessee River, this refuge provides excellent habitats for coots, particularly in its shallow waters and wetlands.

- **Chickamauga Lake**: Near Chattanooga, this reservoir offers diverse aquatic environments where American coots can often be observed.

- **Percy Priest Lake**: Located near Nashville, this lake features wetlands and is a good spot for spotting American coots, especially in winter.

- **Shelby Farms Park**: This large park in Memphis has ponds and wetlands that attract various bird species, including American coots.

- **Land Between the Lakes National Recreation Area**: This area includes lakes and wetlands that are ideal for observing American coots.

OTHER RESOURCES:

Tennessee Wildlife Management Areas: This map is very helpful to find places to watch birds and other wildlife: https://www.tn.gov/content/tn/twra/wildlife-management-areas.html

100 Common Birds of Tennessee: This is a great resource on where to find certain birds in the state: https://www.tn.gov/twra/wildlife/birds/100-birds-of-tennessee.html

Audubon Guide to North American Birds: A great resource from the premier bird advocacy group, the Audubon Society. https://www.audubon.org/bird-guide

The Cornell lab of Ornithology: This is an excellent resource for all things birds from Cornell University. Their app can help identify birds sounds. https://www.birds.cornell.edu/ eBird https://ebird.org/home An online database of bird observations providing scientists, researchers and amateur naturalists with real-time data about bird distribution and abundance.

U.S. Fish and Wildlife Services Birds of Conservation Concern https://www.fws.gov/birds/management/managed-species/birds-of-conservation-concern.php

The National Audubon Society. The National Audubon Society protects birds and the places they need, today and tomorrow, throughout the Americas using science, advocacy, education, and on-the-ground conservation. https://www.audubon.org/

FIELD GUIDES:

National Geographic Society. 2002. Birds of North America, 4th edition. NY: National Geographic

Peterson RT. 2020. Peterson field guide to the birds of eastern and central North America. NY: Houghton Mifflin Harcourt.

Robbins CS. 2001. Golden guide to the birds of North America. MD: St Martin's Press.

Sibley DA. 2016. The Sibley field guide to the birds of North America, 2nd edition. NY: Knopf.

Bird Collisions

To prevent bird collisions with windows, place your feeders more than 30 feet from a window or less than three feet from the window. 30 feet away from a window is a safe distance to prevent collisions caused by reflections wile 3 feet prevents birds from building up the momentum while flying to cause a fatal collision

READ OTHER
50 THINGS TO KNOW ABOUT
BIRDS IN THE UNITED STATES BOOKS

50 Things to Know About Birds in Illinois

50 Things to Know About Birds in Missouri

50 Things to Know About Birds in New York

50 Things to Know About Birds in Oklahoma

50 Things to Know About Birds in Oregon

50 Things to Know About Birds in Pennsylvania

Stay up to date with new releases on Amazon:

https://amzn.to/2VPNGr7

CZYKPublishing.com

Made in the USA
Columbia, SC
21 April 2025

852905fe-e2ea-4cec-abfd-03a2ac327737R01